To my one million readers....

Low Calorie Healthy Cooking

TARLA DALAL

S&C

SANJAY & CO.
BOMBAY

Sixteenth Printing : 2002

Price Rs. 250/-

Published & Distributed by : **Sanjay & Company**

353/A-1 Shah & Nahar Industrial Estate, Dhanraj Mill Compound,
Lower Parel (W), Mumbai - 400 013. INDIA.
Tel. : (91-22) 2496 8068 ● Fax : (91-22) 2496 5876 ● E-mail : sanjay@tarladalal.com

Printed by : **Jupiter Prints**, Mumbai

: Nutritional Guidance :
Dr. Swati Piramal, Ms. Anar Shah

: Art Director :
Pramilla Fonseca

: Photography :
Mr. Rajeev Asgaonkar

OTHER BOOKS BY TARLA DALAL

INDIAN COOKING
Tava Cooking
Rotis & Subzis
Desi Khana
The Complete Gujarati Cook Book
Mithai
Chaat
Achaar aur Parathe
The Rajasthani Cookbook

WESTERN COOKING
The Complete Italian Cookbook
The Chocolate Cookbook
Eggless Desserts
Mocktails & Snacks
Soups & Salads
Mexican Cooking
Easy Gourmet Cooking
Chinese Cooking
Thai Cooking

TOTAL HEALTH
Pregnancy Cookbook
Baby and Toddler Cookbook
Cooking with 1 Teaspoon of Oil
Home Remedies
Delicious Diabetic Recipes

MINI SERIES
A new world of Idlis & Dosas
Cooking under 10 minutes
Pizzas and Pastas
Fun Food for Kids
Roz Ka Khana
Microwave - Desi Khana
T.V. Meals
Fast Food

GENERAL COOKING
Exciting Vegetarian Cooking
Party Cooking
Microwave Cooking
Quick & Easy Cooking
Saatvik Khana
Mixer Cook Book

The Pleasures of Vegetarian Cooking
The Delights of Vegetarian Cooking
The Joys of Vegetarian Cooking
Cooking With Kids
Snacks Under 10 Minutes
Ice-Cream & Frozen Desserts

ISBN No. 81-9000353-2-0

Visit us on our Home Page http://www.tarladalal.com

CONTENTS

continued ...

VI. Western Dishes

VII. Desserts

continued ...

AUTHOR'S NOTE

Despite the availability of numerous books on dieting in the market, most people think that dieting is a difficult task with the prospect of eating dull, monotonous and insipid food like boiled vegetables from day to day. Well, this need not be so. You can reduce weight and at the same time plan your meals from a variety of tasty and healthy vegetarian dishes. You can choose from among Indian, Chinese, Western, Italian and Mexican dishes such as those given in the book.

In my work, I have taken advice and help from the nutritionists and experts at the Human Performance Laboratory of Gopikrishna Piramal Memorial Hospital, Bombay; and have created and modified recipes with a view to achieving the desired nutritional goals. For proper use of this book, read the Nutritional Note by Dr. Swati Piramal and Ms. Anar Shah. The Health Information given as a guide below each recipe should prove of interest. And for readers who are interested in more nutritional particulars, also the chart given at the end of the book.

I would like to take this opportunity to acknowledge the invaluable help of Dr. Swati Piramal and her colleagues in preparing this book.

This book should open new vistas in the field of vegetarian food to dieters and I wish them enjoyable healthy eating.

Tarla Dalal

NUTRITIONAL NOTE

The diet goals of this book are to bring about weight loss as well as ensuring good health by:

1. Keeping fat at a minimum, especially saturated fats.
2. Reducing the amount of sugar consumed.
3. Reducing cholesterol intake.
4. Limiting salt intake; using herbs and spices to reduce salt and bring out the flavours.
5. Increasing consumption of complex carbohydrates.
6. Avoiding processed and preserved foods; instead eating more fresh and natural foods.

All the recipes in this book have been analyzed by the computerized interactive graphic diet analysis programme at The Human Performance Laboratory, Gopikrishna Piramal Memorial Hospital, Bombay. The recipes are low in calories as well as balanced and healthy. Each computer controlled recipe is a comprehensive nutrition analysis of 58 different nutrients which include:

calories	protein	carbohydrates	fat	fibre
cholesterol	fatty acids	sodium	iron	potassium
magnesium	zinc	vit. A	vit. D	vit. C
vit. E	niacin	vit. B1	vit. B2	panto-acid
vit. B6	vit. B12	phosphorus	vit. K	alcohol
copper	manganese	calcium	iodine	caffeine
flouride	selenium	molybdenum	sugar	biotin
chloride	chromium	trytophan	valine	threonine
isoleucine	leucine	methionine	lysine	cystine
phenyl-anine	tyrosine	histidine	ash	

THE ABCS OF NUTRITION

1. PROTEINS

Protein is an indispensable part of the diet, involved in the body's vital functions such as growth, maintenance and repair of cells, for production of enzymes and hormones and for energy. Every protein is made up of amino acids — smaller molecules known as the building blocks of protein. These molecules are combined in many different ways in different foods. The combinations in which protein foods are eaten are very important. Animal source proteins such as milk and milk products and eggs supply all the essential amino acids. Vegetable source proteins such as lentils, beans like soyabeans, moong beans, chick peas are also good sources of protein. Grains like wheat, rice, corn and most vegetables provide some protein. By combining a vegetable protein with an animal protein or two complementary vegetable proteins, our intake of protein or two complementary vegetable proteins, our intake of protein is complete. eg. rice and dal, parathas and dahi, pasta and cheese. A daily consumption of 0.8gms of protein per kg. of body weight (about 45gms for women and 55gms for men) is recommended. This works out to about 10-15 per cent of the daily dietary intake. Each gram protein provides 4 calories.

2. CARBOHYDRATES

Carbohydrates are the principal sources of energy for the body. Not all foods contain the same kind of carbohydrates; the type — simple and complex is important. Simple carbohydrates like sugars produce energy quickly. If taken in excess, they convert to fat, adding undesirable weight. Therefore, foods such as soft drinks, sweets, chocolates and cakes should be avoided. Complex carbohydrates such as whole grains, beans, vegetables and fruits are less likely to add unwanted weight as they contain a lot of water and fibre. They are more filling and much less likely to be eaten in fattening excess. In addition, unlike simple carbohydrates, they provide vitamins, minerals and in many cases proteins. The diet should contain large amounts of complex carbohydrates. Fruits contain fructose which are desirable simple sugars. They have fibre and vitamins as well. The daily diet should contain about 60-65 per cent of carbohydrates. Each gram carbohydrate provides 4 calories.

3. FIBRE

Fibre is sometimes called "nature's broom" because it helps in the elimination of products of digestion. Fibre absorbs moisture, thereby adding bulk and helps to satisfy the appetite. It is found in plant foods like whole grains, beans, peas, fruits and vegetables and should be consumed in adequate amounts.

4. FATS

Fats are an essential part of the diet and a good source of energy. They insulate the body and are carriers of fat soluble vitamins. The body stores all extra calories in the form of fat. Animal fats such as butter and ghee as also vegetable fats like vanaspati, coconut and palm oils are high in saturated fatty acids which are implicated in heart disease. Therefore, their intake should be minimised. Vegetable oils like sunflower, safflower, soyabean, corn and groundnut have a higher amount of unsaturated fatty acids (in the above order) and are preferable to saturated fats. The average urban diet is high in fat and steps must be taken to reduce the fat intake.
Suggestions to help reduce the fat intake are:
1. Use low fat cooking methods like steaming, poaching or baking instead of frying.
2. Use vegetable oils in cooking. Use non-stick vessels.
3. Substitute skim and low fat milk and milk products for whole milk, cream and processed cheese.
The daily dietary intake of fat should be about 15-30 per cent (20-60gms). Each gram fat provides 9 calories.

5. CHOLESTEROL

Cholesterol is essential to the human body in small amounts for the manufacture of hormones. An average diet should contain less than 250-300mg of cholesterol per day. A high level of blood cholesterol increases the risk of heart disease. Eggs and high fat dairy products such as butter, pure ghee, cream, cheese have large amounts of cholesterol and therefore they should be restricted in the daily diet.

6. VITAMINS AND MINERALS

Vitamins and minerals are nutrients, vital in small amounts to life and growth. A prolonged shortage of any of these can lead to a deficiency disease.
Listed below are the main vitamins and minerals and their roles.

VITAMIN	RICH FOOD SOURCES	IMPORTANT BODY FUNCTIONS
VIT. A	carrots, spinach, milk, cheese, peaches, eggs, melon, apricot	maintains eyes, skin, mucous membrane; prevents night blindness; promotes normal growth of bones
VIT. C	citrus fruits, potato, tomato, green vegetables	promotes growth of skin, bones, teeth, tendons; prevents scurvy
VIT. D	milk, eggs	essential for growth and maintenance of strong bones
VIT. K	green leafy vegetables, cauliflower, cereal, fruits	maintains normal blood clotting
VIT. E	vegetable oils, eggs, margarine	essential for blood functioning
VIT. B1	breads, cereals, legumes, leafy vegetables, nuts	aids in transmission of nerve impulses and reactions providing energy
VIT. B2	milk, breads, cereals, green leafy vegetables	promotes helathy skin, nerves & eyes; aids in release of energy
VIT. B6	whole grain cereals, bananas, vegetables	maintains nervous tissues, regenerates red blood cells
VIT. B12	dairy products	required for proper functioning of all cells
NIACIN	grains, breads, nuts, vegetables	helps convert food into energy
FOLACIN	leafy vegetables, eggs, legumes	prevents blood disorders; helps body use proteins

11

MINERAL	RICH FOOD SOURCES	IMPORTANT BODY FUNCTIONS
CALCIUM	milk, cheese, green vegetables, citrus fruits	formation of bones & teeth, blood clotting, heart function
CHROMIUM	vegetable oils, whole-grain cereals & breads	involved in glucose and energy metabolism
COPPER	nuts, whole grains	helps produce haemoglobin
IODINE	iodized salt, milk	proper working of thyroid gland
IRON	leafy green vegetables, beans	essential component of haemoglobin, deficiency causes anaemia
MAGNESIUM	milk, cheese, vegetables, whole grain cereals	activates energy supplying enzymes
PHOSPHORUS	milk, cheese, grains, nuts, legumes	formation of bones & teeth, regulates many body functions
POTASSIUM	oranges, milk, fruits, vegetables	balances water levels in cells
SODIUM	table salt, most foods	regulates fluids in body, thus influences blood pressure; essential to nerve function and energy production. Most diets have an excess of sodium that may lead to high blood pressure
ZINC	eggs, milk	promotes growth of tissues, prevents anaemia

7. WATER

The human body is about 60 per cent water. Of all the essential nutrients, water is the most critical as it is used by every body function. Since water has no calories, it is advantageous for the dieter. Foods such as cucumber, lettuce and watermelon are high in water and therefore low in calories and quite filling. About 6 to 8 glasses of water should be consumed daily.

A reducing diet must be nutritionally balanced, containing adequate amounts of nutrients such as proteins, carbohydrates, fats, minerals and vitamins to ensure good health. It should form the basis for your dietary re-education so that proper eating habits will continue after the desired loss of weight has been obtained. Unbalanced diets by comparison, are those that radically departs from this standard by overloading one group at the expense of others and can easily have a deficiency of important nutrients. They can be dangerous and may impair health over a long range; and therefore are not recommended eg. crash diets, fad diets, water diets, prolonged fasting.

In this book, sample computer controlled, low calorie meals are given which are balanced and cover all the food groups. We have given at the end of each recipe, the relevant health information.

DR. SWATI PIRAMAL, Medical Director
ANAR SHAH, Food and Nutrition Technologist

The Gopikrishna Piramal Memorial Hospital
Off Worli Naka, Bombay 400 025

BIBLIOGRAPHY

1. Agriculture handbooks no. # 8-1 to 8-6 USDA 1977-1986
2. Nutritive value of foods in common units USDA # 456, 1975
3. Recommended Dietary Allowances, National Research Council 1980
4. Nutritive Values Of Indian Foods, C. Gopalan 1982
5. Clinical Dietetics and Nutrition, F.P. Antia 2nd edition
6. Wholesome Diet, Time — Life Publication 1981
7. Eat Better Live Better, Reader's Digest 1982
8. Nutrient Value of Beverages USDA 1982
9. Table of Amino Acids USDA 1983
10. Folacin in Selected Foods USDA 1979

1. Drinks

Frosted Tomato Cocktail

Preparation time: 15 minutes • Cooking time: 5 minutes • Makes 4 glasses.

1 kg. tomatoes
3 teaspoons sugar
a little Worcestershire sauce
salt to taste

1. Chop the tomatoes.
2. Add the remaining ingredients and 4 tablespoons of water and cook for 2 minutes.
3. Blend in a mixer.
4. Pour the mixture into a tray and freeze for 40 minutes.

★ Serve cold in individual glasses.

Health Information: Full of Vitamins A and C, this drink is more refreshing and healthier than a cola.

Per Glass: Calories 60 • Protein 2g • Carbohydrates 13g • Fat 0.5g

Coffee Frappé

PICTURE ON PAGE 127

Preparation time: 2 minutes ● No cooking ● Makes 1 glass.

1 heaped teaspoon instant coffee
2 teaspoons skim milk powder
2 teaspoons sugar
4 ice cubes

1. Blend all the ingredients with ½ teacup of water in a mixer until frothy.
2. Pour into a tall glass.

★ Serve immediately.

Health Information: This frappé contains the adult's chromium requirement for the day. Coffee in small quantities is a stimulant for the nervous system. However, it should not be drunk by children and people with stomach problems.

Per Glass: Calories 52 ● Protein 3.5g ● Carbohydrates 9.5g ● Fat 0g

1. ICY WATERMELON DRINK, page 21
2. MINTY CUCUMBER COOLER, page 22
3. GOLDEN GLOW, page 20

Tomato Apple Drink

PICTURE ON PAGE 117

Preparation time: 5 minutes • Cooking time: 10 minutes • Makes 6 glasses.

6 medium tomatoes
2 large apples
salt to taste

1. Cut the tomatoes into big pieces.
2. Peel the apples and cut into big pieces.
3. Mix the tomatoes and apples with ½ teacup of water and put to cook.
4. When cooked, blend the mixture in a liquidiser. Strain.
5. Chill.

★ Serve chilled with ice cubes.

Health Information: Apples have a high fibre content and are rich in pectin which has the capacity of absorbing matter and increasing intestinal bulk. Apples may be prescribed in diarrhoea.

Per Glass: Calories 40 • Protein 0.7g • Carbohydrates 10g • Fat 0.3g

1. MUSHROOM SOUP, page 30
2. SPINACH SOUP, page 23
3. CARROT SOUP, page 28

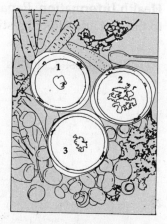

Health Drink

Preparation time: a few minutes • No cooking • Makes 2 glasses.

2 tomatoes
1 carrot
segments of 1 orange
a few drops lemon juice
1 teaspoon sugar
salt and pepper to taste
crushed ice to serve

1. Cut the tomatoes and carrots into big pieces.
2. Add the orange segments, lemon juice, sugar and 1/2 teacup of water and blend in a liquidiser. Strain.
3. Add salt and pepper.

★ Serve cold with crushed ice.

Health Information: This drink is good for the eyes. Its high fibre content also helps to maintain good intestinal movement.

Per Glass: Calories 69 • Protein 2g • Carbohydrates 16g • Fat 1g

Golden Glow

PICTURE ON PAGE 17

Preparation time: 5 minutes • No cooking • Makes 1 tall glass.

1 teacup papaya pieces
1 teaspoon sugar
4 ice cubes

1. To the papaya, add the sugar, ice cubes and ½ cup of water.
2. Blend in a mixer.

★ Serve immediately with ice cubes.

Health Information: Papaya is a rich source of Vitamin A. It also helps to add bulk to the diet and aids digestion.

Per Glass: Calories 42 • Protein 0.5g • Carbohydrates 11g • Fat 0.1g

Icy Watermelon Drink

PICTURE ON PAGE 17

Preparation time: 5 minutes • No cooking • Makes 3 glasses.

3   teacups watermelon pieces
3   teaspoons skim milk powder
1½ teaspoons sugar

1. Blend the ingredients in a liquidiser.
2. Pour into ice cube trays and freeze in the freezer compartment of a refrigerator.

★ When you want to serve, put the frozen mixture in a liquidiser, churn and pour into 3 glasses. If you like, add ice cubes.

Health Information: A cool, refreshing drink using low calorie watermelons. Good for summer parties.

Per Glass: Calories 56 • Protein 2g • Carbohydrates 12g • Fat 0.6g

---

Sunshine Drink

Preparation time: 5 minutes • No cooking • Makes 2 glasses.

2   teacups chopped tomatoes
segments of ½ orange
1   chopped carrot
2   tablespoons papaya cubes *or* melon cubes
a few drops lemon juice
1   teaspoon sugar
2   pinches salt
2   ice cubes

1. Blend all the ingredients in a liquidiser with ½ teacup of water.
2. Strain.

★ Serve immediately.

Health Information: The drink gives all the Vitamins A and C requirement for the day.

Per Glass: Calories 72 • Protein 2g • Carbohydrates 17g • Fat 0.4g

Minty Cucumber Cooler

PICTURE ON PAGE 17

Preparation time: 10 minutes • No cooking • Makes 4 glasses.

1 kg. fresh cucumber
250 grams fresh curds, *page 134*
a few mint leaves
salt to taste

1. Chop one cucumber finely. Cut the remaining cucumbers into big pieces.
2. Add 3 teacups of water to the big cucumber pieces and cook until soft.
3. When soft, blend in a liquidiser. Cool.
4. Add the curds and salt and beat well.
5. Top with crushed ice, mint leaves and the finely chopped cucumber. Alternatively, pound the mint leaves with a dash of green chilli and add to the drink.

   ★ Serve cold.

Health Information: A refreshing drink containing low calorie, Vitamin C rich cucumbers and protein and vitamin-rich curds. The mint leaves, besides adding flavour, provide small quantities of vitamins and iron.

Per Glass: Calories 52 • Protein 4g • Carbohydrates 9g • Fat 0.6g

Fruit Cup

Preparation time: a few minutes • No cooking • Makes 1 cup.

1 tablespoon chopped apple
1 tablespoon chopped grapes
1 tablespoon orange segments
1 tablespoon sweet lime segments
1 tablespoon orange squash
½ teaspoon thick fresh curds, *page 134*, for topping

1. Put the fruit in a serving cup and pour the orange squash on it.
2. Top with curds.

   ★ Serve cold.

Health Information: A light, refreshing starter with fresh fruits for vitamins and minerals. Curds are a healthy substitute for fresh cream.

Per Cup: Calories 60 • Protein 0.5g • Carbohydrates 14.7g • Fat 0.2g

2. Soups

Spinach Soup

PICTURE ON PAGE 18

Preparation time: 10 minutes • Cooking time: 10 minutes • Serves 4.

2 teacups chopped spinach
1 chopped onion
2 teacups skim milk, *page 132*
salt and pepper to taste

1. Cook the spinach and onion in ½ teacup of water until soft.
2. Add the milk and blend in a mixer. Strain.
3. Add salt and pepper.

★ Serve hot, topped with grated paneer.

Variation: LETTUCE SOUP Instead of spinach, use the same quantity of lettuce.

Health Information: Amongst vegetables, spinach has the highest amount of folic acid which is necessary for preventing anaemia. The combination of spinach and milk results in a highly nutritious soup full of vitamins, iron and calcium. Excellent for children.

Per Serving: Calories 55 • Protein 5g • Carbohydrates 9g • Fat 0.3g

Lentil Soup

PICTURE ON PAGE 72

Preparation time: 10 minutes ● Cooking time: 15 minutes ● Serves 6.

¾ teacup masoor dal (washed)
3 sliced onions
4 cloves crushed garlic
½ teaspoon chilli powder
3 tomatoes
2 teaspoons oil
salt to taste

For serving
lemon juice

For garnish
1 tablespoon boiled rice

1. Heat the oil and fry the onions for 1 minute. Add the garlic and chilli powder and fry again for ½ minute.
2. Add 6 teacups of water, the tomatoes, masoor dal and salt and cook in a pressure cooker till the first whistle.
3. When cooked, blend in a mixer.
4. Boil for 5 minutes.

★ Serve hot with lemon juice and garnished with boiled rice.

Health Information: Pulses are an important source of protein containing twice as much protein as the same weight of cereals. The combination of cereals and pulses provides protein of high biological value.

Per Serving: Calories 101 ● Protein 5.5g ● Carbohydrates 16g ● Fat 2g

Cauliflower Soup

PICTURE ON PAGE 53

Preparation time: 10 minutes • Cooking time: 15 minutes • Serves 6.

250 grams cauliflower
1 small chopped onion
3 teacups skim milk, *page 132*
1 teaspoon butter
salt and pepper to taste

1. Put the cauliflower, milk and 3 teacups of water in a vessel and put to boil.
2. When cooked, blend in a liquidiser. Strain.
3. Heat the butter and fry the onion for ½ minute.
4. Add the cauliflower and liquid and boil for 5 minutes.
5. Add salt and pepper.

★ Serve hot. If you like, top with chopped parsley.

Health Information: Cauliflower contains large amounts of Vitamin C and is rich in minerals. The soup also contains fibre which remains unabsorbed and gives a feeling of fullness despite the fewer calories.

Per Serving: Calories 57 • Protein 4.5g • Carbohydrates 8g • Fat 0.8g

Lentil and Spinach Soup

PICTURE ON PAGE 108

Preparation time: 10 minutes ● Cooking time: 20 minutes ● Makes 10 cups.

½ teacup masoor dal
1 teacup chopped spinach
3 sliced onions
3 medium sized tomatoes, cut into big pieces
1 teacup skim milk, *page 132*
2 cloves crushed garlic (optional)
¼ teaspoon chilli powder
salt to taste

For serving
lemon juice

1. Mix the spinach, onions, tomatoes, masoor dal and garlic.
2. Add 7 teacups of water and cook in a pressure cooker for 10 minutes. When cooked, blend in a mixer. Sieve.
3. Heat the milk and add to the soup.
4. Add the chilli powder and salt.

★ Serve hot with lemon juice.

Health Information: Tomatoes are a rich source of Vitamins A, C and potassium. Combined with spinach which contains iron and calcium, and masoor dal which contains essential amino acids and with milk, they make a nourishing combination.

Per Serving: Calories 48 ● Protein 3.5g ● Carbohydrates 9g ● Fat 0.3g

Chinese Clear Vegetable Soup

PICTURE ON PAGE 107

Preparation time: 10 minutes • Cooking time: 5 minutes • Serves 6.

1 carrot
1 teacup cabbage leaves
3 lettuce leaves
3 spring onions (with leaves)
3 sticks celery
50 grams sliced cauliflower
2 tablespoons refined oil
a pinch baking powder
a pinch citric acid
2 teaspoons soya sauce
salt to taste
green chillies in vinegar and chilli sauce
   to serve

1. Slice the carrot thinly.
2. Tear the cabbage and lettuce leaves.
3. Chop the spring onions with the leaves.
4. Cut the celery into about 12mm. pieces.
5. Heat the oil thoroughly. Add the vegetables, baking powder and citric acid and cook on a high flame for 3 to 4 minutes.
6. Add 5 teacups of boiling water, the soya sauce and salt and boil for 3 to 4 minutes.

★ Serve hot with chillies in vinegar and chilli sauce.

Health Information: This soup uses the stir frying technique (an Oriental method of cooking using small quantities of oil) for cooking whilst stirring over a high flame. This results in minimum loss of nutrients and minimum absorption of fat, making it a very useful nutrient saving cooking technique.

Per Serving: Calories 63 • Protein 1g • Carbohydrates 4g • Fat 5g

Carrot Soup

PICTURE ON PAGE 18

Preparation time: 5 minutes ● Cooking time: 15 minutes ● Makes 5 cups.

400 grams carrots
1 onion
1 tablespoon moong dal
1 teacup skim milk, *page 132*
salt and pepper to taste

1. Cut the carrots and onion into big pieces.
2. Add 3 teacups of water and the moong dal and cook in a pressure cooker.
3. When cooked, blend in a liquidiser and strain.
4. Heat the milk and add to the soup. Mix well.
5. Add salt and pepper and boil for 1 minute.

★ Serve hot.

Health Information: Carrots have a large amount of carotene which helps to form Vitamin A. The soup is enriched with milk and dal to increase the protein value.

Per Serving: Calories 60 ● Protein 3g ● Carbohydrates 12g ● Fat 0.3g

Moong Dal and Spinach Soup

Preparation time: a few minutes ● Cooking time: 15 minutes ● Serves 6.

2 tablespoons moong dal
1 teacup chopped spinach
1 teacup skim milk, *page 132*
salt to taste

1. Add 4 teacups of water to the moong dal and put to cook in a pressure cooker.
2. Add the spinach, milk and salt and boil for 5 to 10 minutes.

★ Serve hot.

Health Information: Rich in Vitamins A and K, essential amino acids and folic acid, this healthy soup is low in calories and is an appropriate accompaniment to a heavier main dish.

Per Serving: Calories 21 ● Protein 3g ● Carbohydrates 5g ● Fat 0.3g

Gazpacho

PICTURE ON PAGE 90

Preparation time: 30 minutes • No cooking • Serves 6 to 8.

1½ kg. tomatoes
¾ teaspoon Worcestershire sauce
¾ teaspoon chilli sauce
1   clove garlic (optional)
2   teaspoons sugar
salt to taste

Accompaniments
1   finely chopped capsicum
1   finely chopped large onion
1   finely chopped cucumber
1   finely chopped tomato

1. Put the tomatoes in boiling water for 10 minutes. Thereafter, remove the skins and chop.
2. Blend in a liquidiser and strain.
3. Add the Worcestershire sauce, chilli sauce, garlic, sugar and salt.
4. Chill thoroughly.

★ Serve cold in cups with accompaniments in separate cups.

Health Information: This recipe is rich in Vitamins A, C and K, chromium, fibre and complex carbohydrates. The cold soup is a refreshing summer starter with the goodness of vitamin-rich tomatoes and raw vegetables.

Per Serving: Calories 59 • Protein 2g • Carbohydrates 12.5g • Fat 0.5g

Clear Vegetable Broth

Preparation time: 10 minutes ● Cooking time: 25 minutes ● Makes 4 cups.

2 thick pieces celery
1 large carrot
1 onion
2 tablespoons chopped parsley
1 bay leaf
6 teacups water
1 teaspoon Marmite
2 teaspoons butter *or* oil
salt and pepper to taste

1. Chop the celery and carrot finely. Cut the onion into rings.
2. Heat the butter, add the bay leaf and onion and cook for 1 minute.
3. Add the vegetables and cook again for 3 to 4 minutes.
4. Add the water and boil for 15 to 20 minutes.
5. Add the chopped parsley, Marmite and salt and pepper.

   ★ Serve hot.

Health Information: A light soup which is very rich in vitamins, especially Vitamin A.

Per Serving: Calories 77 ● Protein 1g ● Carbohydrates 13g ● Fat 2.3g

Mushroom Soup

PICTURE ON PAGE 18

Preparation time: 10 minutes ● Cooking time: 10 minutes ● Makes 5 cups.

200 grams fresh button mushrooms
1 chopped onion
2 teaspoons butter
salt and pepper to taste

1. Chop the mushrooms.
2. Heat the butter and fry the mushrooms and onion for 1 minute.
3. Add 4 teacups of water and put to cook.
4. When cooked, blend in a liquidiser.
5. Add salt and pepper to taste.

   ★ Serve hot.

Health Information: A soup for mushroom lovers. Mushrooms are very low in calories and have a good protein value

Per Serving: Calories 31 ● Protein 1g ● Carbohydrates 3.3g ● Fat 1.8g

Curd Shorba

Preparation time: 10 minutes • Cooking time: 10 minutes • Serves 4.

4 teacups fresh curds, *page 134*
1 teaspoon plain flour
¼ teaspoon turmeric powder
2 tablespoons skim milk, *page 132*
2 teaspoons ghee
½ teaspoon cumin seeds
½ onion, finely chopped (optional)
2 chopped green chillies
½ teaspoon grated ginger (optional)
2 to 4 teaspoons chopped tomatoes
1 tablespoon chopped cucumber
1 tablespoon chopped coriander for
   topping

1. Beat the curds, plain flour, turmeric powder and milk together.
2. Heat the ghee and fry the cumin seeds until they crackle.
3. Add the onion, green chillies and ginger and fry again for a few seconds.
4. Add the curds mixture and boil for a few minutes. Add the tomatoes and cucumber and cook for 1 minute.
5. Top with the chopped coriander.

★ Serve hot.

Health Information: Curds help produce vitamins and inhibit growth of disease producing bacteria in the intestines.

Per Serving: Calories 98 • Protein 8.5g • Carbohydrates 8g • Fat 3g

Mixed Vegetable Soup

Preparation time: 10 minutes • Cooking time: 10 minutes • Serves 6.

4 chopped tomatoes
2 tablespoons chopped cabbage
2 tablespoons chopped capsicum
2 tablespoons chopped onion
2 bay leaves
2 teaspoons oil
salt and pepper to taste

1. Heat the oil and fry the onion for 1 minute.
2. Add the tomatoes, cabbage, capsicum, bay leaves and 6 teacups of boiling water and boil for 5 minutes.
3. Add salt and pepper.

★ Serve hot.

Health Information: A vitamin-rich soup that is light and very low in calories. Serve with a heavier main dish.

Per Serving: Calories 27 • Protein 0.5g • Carbohydrates 2.5g • Fat 1.8g

Cold Cucumber Soup

Preparation time: 10 minutes ● Cooking time: 10 minutes ● Serves 6.

1 kg. fresh cucumber
½ litre fresh curds, *page 134*
1 teacup skim milk, *page 132*
1 tablespoon chopped capsicum
1 tablespoon butter
salt to taste
a few mint leaves for topping (optional)

1. Chop one cucumber finely. Cut the remaining cucumbers into big pieces.
2. Add 3 teacups of water to the big cucumber pieces and cook until soft.
3. When soft, blend in a liquidiser. Cool.
4. Add the curds, milk and salt and beat well.
5. Heat the butter and fry the finely chopped cucumber and the capsicum for ½ minute. Add to the soup.
6. Chill.

How to serve
Pour the soup into big individual bowls and add 1 to 2 ice cubes.

★ Top with chopped mint leaves and serve.

Health Information: Cucumbers are one of the lowest calorie vegetables with a lot of Vitamin C and potassium. One can never get fat eating cucumbers as they contain 96 per cent water.

Per Serving: Calories 76 ● Protein 5g ● Carbohydrates 9g ● Fat 2.6g

Vegetable Soup

Preparation time: 15 minutes • Cooking time: 25 minutes • Serves 6.

For the stock
2 tablespoons moong dal
2 onions
2 large tomatoes

Other ingredients
1 chopped onion
1 shredded carrot
½ teacup shredded cabbage
½ teacup chopped spinach
1 tablespoon tomato ketchup
1 chopped tomato
2 teaspoons oil
salt and pepper to taste

For serving
3 tablespoons grated cheese

For the stock
1. Cut the onions and tomatoes into big pieces.
2. Add the moong dal and 6 teacups of water and cook in a pressure cooker till the first whistle.
3. When cooked, blend in a liquidiser and strain.

How to proceed
1. Heat the oil and fry the onion for 1 minute.
2. Add the stock, carrot, cabbage and spinach and boil for 10 minutes.
3. Add the ketchup, chopped tomato, salt and pepper and boil for 10 minutes.

★ Serve hot with grated cheese.

Health Information: A hearty soup with an Italian flavour. The dal combined with the vegetables give the complete protein requirements. Rich in Vitamins A, C, B and K and essential amino acids.

Per Serving: Calories 89 • Protein 4g • Carbohydrates 10g • Fat 4g

Green Peas Skin Soup

Preparation time: 10 minutes • Cooking time: 10 minutes • Serves 6.

6 teacups skin of green peas
1 tablespoon green peas
1 chopped onion
3 teacups skim milk, *page 132*
2 teaspoons butter
salt and pepper to taste

1. Heat the butter and fry the onion for 1 minute.
2. Add the green peas skin and green peas and cook for 3 to 4 minutes.
3. Add the milk and ½ teacup of water and cook in a pressure cooker till the first whistle.
4. Blend in a mixer.
5. Strain to separate the stock from the skin. Discard the skin.
6. Boil the stock for 1 minute.
7. Add salt and pepper.

★ Serve hot.

Health Information: This unusual soup gives the flavour of peas without the calories. Fresh green pea pods add fibre and Vitamins A and C to the soup. Fibre is called nature's broom because it helps sweep the products of digestion through the body and eliminates them.

Per Serving: Calories 55 • Protein 4g • Carbohydrates 6.5g • Fat 1.5g

1. FRUITY BEAN SALAD, page 40

3. Salads

Slimmers' Salad

PICTURE ON PAGE 108

Preparation time: 10 minutes ● No cooking ● Serves 8.

4   dessert apples
1   fresh pear (optional)
segments of 1 orange
1   medium sized capsicum
4   carrots
4   sticks celery
½ cucumber
a few raisins

1. Chop the fruits coarsely.
2. Grate the vegetables.
3. Mix in a bowl and put to chill.
4. If you like, add the curd dressing.

★ Serve cold

Note: The curd dressing contains 38 calories.

Accompaniment
1   teacup curd dressing, *page 45*

Health Information: This delicious salad contains all the Vitamins A and C needed in the full day's diet. Vitamin A is good for the eyes and a glowing complexion. Eating fruits and vegetables uncooked preserves both bulk and nutrient content.

Per Serving: Calories 72 ● Protein 1g ● Carbohydrates 18g ● Fat 0.4g

INDIAN BREAKFAST
1. BUTTER MILK, one glass
2. MOONG DAL DHOKLAS, three pieces, page 65
3. PANEER PALAK METHI ROTI, one serving, page 62
4. APPLE, one

Health information: A meal rich in essential amino acids, iron, calcium and phosphorus. This high protein breakfast provides a good start for the day.

Per Breakfast: Calories 286 ● Protein 16g ● Carbohydrates 53g ● Fat 3.2g

Sprouted Moong Salad

PICTURE ON PAGE 53

Preparation time: 15 minutes • Cooking time: 5 minutes • Serves 6.

2 teacups sprouted moong, *page 131*
2 chopped tomatoes
1 tablespoon chopped coriander
1 chopped green chilli
2 teaspoons lemon juice
1 teaspoon sugar
1 teacup chopped cabbage
½ teacup grated carrots
1 chopped onion (optional)
salt to taste

1. Steam the sprouted moong for 5 minutes.
2. Add the remaining ingredients, mix well and put to chill.

★ Serve cold.

Health Information: A power packed protein-rich salad which is excellent for people on the go. Rich in complex carbohydrates and vitamins.

Per Serving: Calories 63 • Protein 4g • Carbohydrates 12g • Fat 0.2g

Bean Sprouts Salad

PICTURE ON PAGE 72

Preparation time: 5 minutes ● No cooking ● Serves 4.

2 teacups bean sprouts, *page 136*
2 sliced onions
2 sliced tomatoes
a few drops soya sauce (optional)
salt to taste

1. Mix the sprouts, onions, tomatoes and salt.
2. If you like, sprinkle a little soya sauce on top.
3. Chill.

★ Serve cold.

Health Information: Together, moong and soya give a nutritive high protein salad. Furthermore, raw sprouts and vegetables increase the fibre content as well as prevent loss of nutrients.

Per Serving: Calories 85 ● Protein 5g ● Carbohydrates 15g ● Fat 0.5g

---

Stuffed Capsicums

Preparation time: 10 minutes ● No cooking ● Serves 4.

2 capsicums
1 teacup thick fresh curds, *page 134*
1 teacup grated cucumber
1 chopped green chilli
salt to taste

1. Tie the curds in a thin muslin cloth. Hang and allow the water to drain out. When thick, place in a bowl.
2. Squeeze out the water from the cucumber and add to the curds.
3. Add the green chilli and salt.
4. Divide each capsicum into two and scoop out the centres. Fill with the curds mixture and chill.

★ Serve cold.

Health Information: Capsicums which are an excellent source of Vitamin C are mildly flavoured and do not cause gastric irritation. A good accompaniment to a heavier dish.

Per Serving: Calories 31 ● Protein 3g ● Carbohydrates 5g ● Fat 0.5g

Fruity Bean Salad

PICTURE ON PAGE 35

Preparation time: 20 minutes • Cooking time: 30 minutes • Serves 8.

175 grams mixed boiled sprouted pulses
    (green grams, math, chick peas, green
    peas etc.) *page 131*
1   teacup chopped apples
segments of 1 orange
2   tablespoons cut grapes
2   tablespoons sliced white radish
1   teacup chopped salad leaves
½ teacup chopped spinach leaves
1   finely chopped green chilli (optional)
salt to taste

1. Mix all the ingredients except dressing thoroughly.
2. Put to chill.
3. Just before serving, top the salad with the dressing.

★ Serve chilled.

To be mixed into a dressing
1   teacup fresh curds, *page 134*
2   tablespoons chopped mint leaves
1   teaspoon sugar
salt to taste

Health Information: This combination of pulses which provide proteins (and B group vitamins), fruits which provide Vitamins A and C and leafy green vegetables which provide iron and calcium, accompanied by a dairy curd dressing makes this an extremely healthy salad.

Per Serving: Calories 62 • Protein 4g • Carbohydrates 11g • Fat 0.5g

Fruity Vegetable Salad

Preparation time: 15 minutes ● No cooking ● Serves 6.

For the fruits and vegetables
2 teacups watermelon pieces
1 teacup fresh pineapple pieces
2 tablespoons cut grapes (optional)
1 tablespoon chopped celery
2 medium cucumbers, cut into small
   pieces
1 chopped capsicum

For the fruits and vegetables
1. Mix the cut fruits and vegetable
   pieces.
2. Chill.

For the curds parsley dressing
1½ teacups fresh curds, *page 134*
2 tablespoons chopped parsley
½ teaspoon mustard powder (optional)
½ teaspoon sugar
½ teaspoon salt

For the curds parsley dressing
1. Tie the curds in a thin muslin cloth.
   Hang for 1 hour and allow the water
   to drain out.
2. Add the remaining ingredients and
   blend in a mixer.

For decoration
a few lettuce leaves

How to proceed
Put the salad in a bowl. Top with the
dressing and decorate by surrounding
with lettuce leaves.

★ Serve cold.

Health Information: A delightful healthy combination of fresh fruits and
vegetables with a protein and vitamin-rich dressing.

Per Serving: Calories 53 ● Protein 3g ● Carbohydrates 11g ● Fat 0.6g

Orange and Cabbage Salad

Preparation time: 10 minutes • Cooking time: 5 minutes • Serves 10.

9 teaspoons chopped China grass
juice of 8 oranges
¼ teaspoon lemon juice
2 teaspoons sugar
1 teacup shredded cabbage
½ teacup grated carrot
2 tablespoons chopped celery
2 tablespoons chopped capsicum
segments of 1 orange
salt to taste
grated cabbage and carrot
    for decoration

For serving
Thousand Island curds dressing, *page 44*

1. Put the vegetables in cold water for 10 minutes. Drain.
2. Add 1 teacup of water to the China grass and cook on a slow flame until it dissolves completely. Strain.
3. Add the orange juice and boil for 1 minute.
4. Cool until lukewarm and then add the lemon juice, sugar, vegetables, orange segments and salt. Place in an attractive mould and put to set in the refrigerator.
5. Just before serving, dip the mould in hot water for a few seconds, loosen the sides and unmould on a plate. Decorate with grated cabbage and carrots.

★ Serve with Thousand Island curds dressing.

Health Information: Cabbage is rich in Vitamins A and C, calcium, phosphorous and potassium. Oranges are rich in Vitamins A and C and minerals. Together, they make a salad rich in vitamins and minerals.

Per Serving: Calories 52 • Protein 1g • Carbohydrates 13g • Fat 0.2g

4. Dips, Dressings and Raita

Curd Cheese Dip

PICTURE ON PAGE 117

Preparation time: 10 minutes • No cooking • Serves 4.

2 teacups thick fresh curds, *page 134*
2 teaspoons chopped onions
3 teaspoons chopped celery
4 teaspoons chopped capsicum
1 teaspoon salt

Accompaniment
capsicum sticks *or* carrot sticks

1. Tie the curds in a thin muslin cloth. Hang and allow the water to drain out for 1 hour.
2. Add the remaining ingredients and mix well.

★ Serve cold with capsicum sticks or carrot sticks.

Note: Each capsicum or carrot stick contains less than 1 calorie.

Health Information: This low-calorie cheese dip is a tasty substitute for cheese and cream dips which are high in fat and cholesterol.

Per Serving: Calories 34 • Protein 4g • Carbohydrates 3.5g • Fat 0.5g

Fruit and Vegetable Raita

PICTURE ON PAGE 54

Preparation time: 10 minutes ● No cooking ● Serves 7.

1 teacup fresh curds, *page 134*
1 teacup chopped apples
1 chopped cucumber
½ teacup chopped raw cabbage
1 teaspoon sugar
1 chopped green chilli
2 tablespoons cut grapes
salt to taste

1. Beat the curds.
2. Mix the remaining ingredients.
3. Put in the refrigerator to cool.

★ Serve cold.

Health Information: A dish with the goodness of fresh curds combined with vitamins and mineral rich fruits and vegetables.

Per Serving: Calories 27 ● Protein 1g ● Carbohydrates 6g ● Fat 0.3g

Thousand Island Curds Dressing

Preparation time: 10 minutes ● No cooking ● Serves 8.

¾ teacup thick fresh curds, *page 134*
1 teaspoon mustard powder
1 teaspoon sugar
3 tablespoons tomato ketchup
1 teaspoon chilli sauce
2 teaspoons chopped onion
2 teaspoons chopped capsicum
½ teaspoon chopped green chilli
1 teaspoon salt

1. Mix all the ingredients thoroughly.
2. Use the same day.

Health Information: The delicious taste of Thousand Island dressing without the calories and the cholesterol of cream. What is more, your guests will hardly notice the difference.

Per Serving: Calories 15 ● Protein 0.8g ● Carbohydrates 3g ● Fat 0.1g

Spinach Raita

Preparation time: 10 minutes • Cooking time: 10 minutes • Serves 5.

100 grams chopped spinach
1   teacup fresh curds, *page 134*
¼   teaspoon chilli-ginger paste
salt and pepper to taste

1. Steam the spinach.
2. Beat the curds. Add the chilli-ginger paste, salt and pepper and mix well.
3. Add the spinach and mix thoroughly.
4. Put in the refrigerator to cool.

★ Serve cold.

Health Information: A protein rich accompaniment to parathas. Full of vitamins and minerals.

Per Serving: Calories 18 • Protein 2g • Carbohydrates 2g • Fat 0.2g

Curd Dressing

Preparation time: 30 minutes • No cooking • Makes 2 cups.

2   teacups thick fresh curds, *page 134*
1   tablespoon chopped onions
½   teaspoon chopped green chilli
1   teaspoon mustard powder
1   teaspoon sugar
salt to taste

1. Tie the curds in a thin muslin cloth. Hang and allow the water to drain out for 1 hour.
2. Add the remaining ingredients.

★ Chill and serve with any fruit or vegetable salad.

Health Information: A dressing rich in proteins, vitamins and minerals which will increase the nutritive value and taste of any salad. It is far healthier than the high cholesterol, high-calorie mayonnaise or salad cream.

Per Cup: Calories 76 • Protein 8g • Carbohydrates 9g • Fat 1g

Eggplant Dip

Preparation time: 5 minutes • Cooking time: 15 minutes • Serves 8.

½ kg. medium eggplant (brinjals)
2 chopped tomatoes
3 tablespoons finely chopped parsley
1 clove garlic, finely crushed
1 teaspoon lemon juice
1 small onion, finely chopped
1 teaspoon cumin powder
salt and pepper to taste

Accompaniment
baked puris, *page 116* (optional)

1. Grill or burn the eggplant on the gas until soft. Peel, wash and mash.
2. Add 1 chopped tomato and blend in a mixer until soft.
3. Place the mixture in a serving bowl, add the remaining ingredients and mix well.

★ Serve with baked puris.

Note: 1 baked puri contains 13 calories.

Health Information: This low calorie dip using eggplant flavoured with herbs and spices is rich in iron and Vitamin C.

Per Serving: Calories 27 • Protein 1g • Carbohydrates 6g • Fat 0.4g

5. Indian Dishes

Baked Vegetable Jalfrazie

Preparation time: 15 minutes • Cooking time: 30 minutes • Serves 8.

2 teacups chopped mixed boiled vegetables (french beans, carrots, cauliflower, green peas)
2 chopped onions
4 tablespoons chopped capsicum
2 chopped tomatoes
½ to 1 teaspoon chilli powder
a pinch garam masala
2 tablespoons chopped coriander
4 tablespoons grated paneer, *page 135*, plus a little extra for topping
1½ teacups tomato gravy, *page 130*
4 teaspoons oil
salt to taste

1. Heat the oil and fry the onions for ½ minute.
2. Add the capsicum and tomatoes and fry again for 2 minutes.
3. Add the vegetables, chilli powder, garam masala, coriander and salt and cook for a few minutes.
4. Spread the tomato gravy on top and sprinkle a little grated paneer over it.
5. Bake in a hot oven at 200°C for 10 minutes.

★ Serve hot.

Health Information: This recipe uses baking, a superior technique of cooking, instead of sautéing or frying in oil.

Per Serving: Calories 86 • Protein 4g • Carbohydrates 9g • Fat 3.8g

Spinach and Vegetable Delight

Preparation time: 10 minutes ● Cooking time: 10 minutes ● Serves 6.

4 teacups chopped spinach
2 tablespoons gram (chana) dal
100 grams chopped mixed boiled
    vegetables (french beans, carrots,
    cauliflower, green peas)
1 chopped tomato
1 chopped onion
25mm. piece ginger, minced
½ teaspoon turmeric powder
1 teaspoon coriander powder
1 teaspoon chilli powder
2 teaspoons oil
salt to taste

1. Soak the dal in water for 3 hours. Drain.
2. Heat the oil and fry the onion for 3 minutes.
3. Add the vegetables and tomato and fry again for 3 minutes.
4. Add the ginger, turmeric, coriander and chilli powders and salt and mix well.
5. Add the soaked dal and cook for 2 minutes.
6. Add the spinach and cook for 2 minutes while stirring continually.
7. Cook the mixture in a pressure cooker until 2 whistles.
8. Beat the mixture with an egg-beater.

★ Serve hot.

Health Information: This recipe contains an excellent combination of proteins from gram dal, the goodness of iron from spinach and the fibre and vitamins from other vegetables.

Per Serving: Calories 66 ● Protein 4g ● Carbohydrates 9g ● Fat 2.4g

Paneer Methi Palak

PICTURE ON PAGE 54

Preparation time: 10 minutes ● Cooking time: 20 minutes ● Serves 5.

3 teacups chopped spinach
1 teacup fresh fenugreek (methi) leaves
a pinch soda bi-carb
25mm. piece ginger
1 chopped onion
3 chopped green chillies
100 grams sliced paneer, *page 135*
3 teaspoons oil
salt to taste

1. Chop the spinach and fenugreek leaves finely.
2. Add 2 teaspoons of water and the soda bi-carb and cook on a slow flame until soft.
3. When cooked, drain out the water and blend the leaves in a liquidiser.
4. Chop the ginger finely.
5. Heat the oil and fry the onion for 1 minute.
6. Add the green chillies and ginger and fry again for a few seconds.
7. Add the blended leaves, paneer and salt.

★ Serve hot.

Health Information: Green leafy vegetables contain Vitamins A and C and iron and form an important part of a balanced diet. The paneer provides high quality protein.

Per Serving: Calories 88 ● Protein 9g ● Carbohydrates 6.5g ● Fat 3.6g

Dal with Spinach

PICTURE ON PAGE 54

Preparation time: 10 minutes ● Cooking time: 25 minutes ● Serves 8.

¾ teacup uncooked moong dal *or* masoor dal
1 chopped onion
1 teaspoon cumin seeds
1 teacup chopped spinach
2 teaspoons amchur powder
1 chopped tomato
½ teaspoon turmeric powder
4 teaspoons oil
salt to taste

To be ground into a paste
6 cloves garlic
3 green chillies
25mm. piece ginger

1. Cook the dal in 3 teacups of water.
2. Heat the oil, add the onion and cumin seeds and fry for 2 minutes.
3. Add the cooked dal, the spinach, amchur powder, tomato, turmeric powder, paste and salt and boil for 5 minutes.

★ Serve hot.

Health Information: This recipe of dal enriched with spinach is a very good source of protein. The garlic used for flavouring is known for its medicinal properties and acts as an antibacterial agent.

Per Serving: Calories 90 ● Protein 5g ● Carbohydrates 12g ● Fat 2.9g

Nawabi Curry

Preparation time: 25 minutes ● Cooking time: 15 minutes ● Serves 6.

3 large tomatoes
100 grams finely chopped mixed boiled
  vegetables (french beans, carrots,
  cauliflower)
½ teaspoon sugar
1 tablespoon oil
salt to taste

To be ground into a paste
1 large onion
1 tablespoon coriander seeds
1 tablespoon cumin seeds
1 tablespoon khus-khus
2 teaspoons aniseed
25mm. piece ginger
2 green chillies
3 cardamoms
3 cloves
3 sticks cinnamon

Accompaniment
plain parathas, *page 56*

1. Chop the tomatoes. Add 1½ teacups of water and cook until soft.
2. Pass through a sieve to make a tomato purée.
3. Heat the oil and fry the paste for 2 to 3 minutes.
4. Add the tomato purée, vegetables, sugar and salt.

★ Serve hot with plain parathas, *page 56*.

Note: Each plain paratha contains 54 calories.

Health Information: A royal curry that is low in calories and goes wonderfully with parathas. A combination of herbs and spices brings out the taste with less salt.

Per Serving: Calories 66 ● Protein 2g ● Carbohydrates 7g ● Fat 3.9g

Tomato and Cauliflower Curry

Preparation time: 10 minutes • Cooking time: 30 minutes • Makes 6 cups.

½ kg. tomatoes
¼ kg. cauliflower
4 teaspoons gram flour (besan)
10 guar *or* clustered beans, cut into pieces
10 okra (ladies' fingers), cut into big
  pieces
2 tablespoons sliced white pumpkin
  (lauki)
2 slit green chillies
½ teaspoon chilli powder
½ teaspoon mustard seeds
½ teaspoon cumin seeds
a pinch asafoetida
2 teaspoons oil
salt to taste

1. Cook the tomatoes and cauliflower in 6 teacups of water until soft. Blend in a mixer.
2. Mix the gram flour with ¼ teacup of water and add to the mixture.
3. Add the remaining vegetables, green chillies, chilli powder and salt and boil for 15 minutes.
4. Heat the oil and fry the mustard seeds and cumin seeds until they crackle. Add the asafoetida.
5. Add to the mixture and boil again for 5 minutes.

★ Serve hot.

Health Information: Rich in fibre, this recipe contains pumpkin and guar which add to the nutrient value. Guar has the effect of reducing blood sugar and may be used as an additive to flour for diabetics.

Per Serving: Calories 67 • Protein 3g • Carbohydrates 10g • Fat 2.4g

INDIAN LUNCH
1. SPROUTED MOONG SALAD, one serving, page 38
2. CURDS, one cup, page 134
3. CABBAGE PARATHAS, two, page 56 + page 58
4. CAULIFLOWER SOUP, one cup, page 25
5. PEAR, one

Health information: This lunch provides almost 50 per cent of protein and fibre and all the Vitamin C and calcium required for the day. It is tasty yet simple to prepare and may be carried to office or school.

Per Lunch: Calories 369 • Protein 22g • Carbohydrates 62g • Fat 5.4g

Brinjal Bhurta

PICTURE ON PAGE 54

Preparation time: 5 minutes • Cooking time: 15 minutes • Serves 4.

½ kg. large round brinjals
1 chopped onion
1 teaspoon finely chopped green chilli
1 chopped tomato
2 teaspoons oil
salt to taste

1. Grill the brinjals on a fire until they become black in colour. Remove the skin and mash thoroughly.
2. Heat the oil and fry the onion for ½ minute.
3. Add the green chilli and fry again for a few seconds.
4. Add the tomato and fry again for 2 minutes.
5. Add the mashed brinjals and salt.

★ Serve hot.

Variation: BHURTA SALAD Add ½ teacup beaten fresh curds, *page 134,* and a pinch of sugar to the above mixture. Serve cold as a salad.

Health Information: A light dish for the brinjal lover. Rich in vitamins and minerals.

Per Serving: Calories 69 • Protein 2g • Carbohydrates 10g • Fat 2.8g

INDIAN DINNER
1. SUJI IDLIS, seven pieces, page 64
2. ROTIS, two
3. BRINJAL BHURTA, one serving, page 55
4. SANDESH WITH GOLDEN APPLES, one serving, page 104
5. FRUIT AND VEGETABLE RAITA, one serving, page 44
6. PANEER METHI PALAK, one serving, page 49
7. DAL WITH SPINACH, one serving, page 50

Health information: A complete Indian meal rich in many nutrients. Unlike most traditional meals, it is low in fats and cholesterol as frying and the use of whole milk products are avoided.

Per Dinner: Calories 448 • Protein 27g • Carbohydrates 81g • Fat 8g

Plain Parathas

PICTURE ON PAGE 53

Preparation time: 10 minutes • Cooking time: a few minutes • Makes 12 thin parathas.

For the dough
1 teacup whole wheat flour
¼ teaspoon salt
1 teaspoon oil

For cooking
2 teaspoons melted butter

Accompaniment
1 teacup fresh curds, *page 134*

For the dough
1. Mix all the ingredients and enough water to make a soft dough.
2. Divide the dough into 12 portions and roll out each portion into very thin 150mm. diameter rounds.

How to proceed
1. Cook on a tawa (griddle) very lightly for a few seconds.
2. Put a portion of the desired stuffing in each paratha and fold. Arrange on a greased baking tray.
3. Brush the parathas lightly with butter and bake in a hot oven at 200°C until light pink in colour (about 5 minutes). Alternatively, cook on a tawa (griddle) on both sides and brush lightly with butter or oil.

★ Serve hot with curds.

Note: 1 teacup fresh curds contains 63 calories i.e. 5 calories per serving.

Health Information: Whole grain flour contains more vitamins, minerals and fibre as compared to highly refined flour where most of the vitamins and minerals are destroyed during processing. When parathas or chapaties are combined with a small amount of pulses and beans or with a dairy product like curds, the amino acids in these complement each other to give a higher quality of protein.

Per Paratha: Calories 54 • Protein 2g • Carbohydrates 9g • Fat 1.5g

Spinach Stuffing for Plain Parathas

Preparation time: 10 minutes • Cooking time: 5 minutes • For 12 parathas.

4 teacups finely chopped spinach
2 chopped onions
2 chopped green chillies
4 tablespoons crumbled paneer, *page 135*
2 teaspoons oil
salt to taste

1. Heat the oil and fry the onions for ½ minute. Add the green chillies and fry again for a few seconds.
2. Add the spinach and cook for 2 minutes.
3. Drain the water, if any.
4. Add the paneer and salt.

Health Information: Spinach is a good source of folic acid, Vitamin A, iron and calcium and is good for growing children.

Per Paratha: Calories 25 • Protein 2g • Carbohydrates 2.5g • Fat 1g

---

Cauliflower Stuffing for Plain Parathas

Preparation time: 10 minutes • Cooking time: a few minutes • For 12 parathas.

2 teacups grated cauliflower
½ teaspoon cumin seeds
1 chopped onion
2 chopped green chillies
1 teaspoon chilli powder (optional)
1 tablespoon chopped coriander
2 teaspoons oil
salt to taste

1. Heat the oil and fry the cumin seeds for ½ minute.
2. Add the onion, green chillies and fry again for ½ minute.
3. Add the cauliflower and salt, sprinkle a little water and cook until three-quarters cooked.
4. Add the chilli powder and coriander and mix well.

Health Information: A tasty filling which will increase the Vitamin C and fibre content of parathas.

Per Paratha: Calories 15 • Protein 0.5g • Carbohydrates 1.5g • Fat 0.9g

Cabbage Stuffing for Plain Parathas

Preparation time: 10 minutes • No cooking • For 12 parathas.

3 teacups finely chopped cabbage
2 tablespoons crumbled panner, *page 135*
1 chopped green chilli
2 tablespoons chopped coriander
salt to taste

1. Sprinkle 1 teaspoon of salt over the cabbage. Leave for 10 minutes and then squeeze out the water.
2. Add the remaining ingredients and mix well.

Health Information: Besides being one of the best sources of Vitamin C, cabbage also provides calcium, phosphorous and potassium. It is good for growing children.

Per Paratha: Calories 10 • Protein 1g • Carbohydrates 2g • Fat 0g

---

Chinese Stuffing for Plain Parathas

Preparation time: 10 minutes • Cooking time: 5 minutes • For 10 parathas.

1 teacup coarsely grated carrots
1½ teacups shredded cabbage
4 tablespoons bean sprouts, *page 136*, (optional)
1 sliced onion
a pinch baking powder
a few drops soya sauce
a pinch sugar
1 tablespoon oil
salt to taste

1. Heat the oil on a high flame.
2. Add the carrots, cabbage, bean sprouts, onion and baking powder and cook on a high flame for 3 to 4 minutes.
3. Add the soya sauce, sugar and salt.

Health Information: A paratha stuffing with an Oriental flavour using the nutrient saving stir-frying method of cooking.

Per Paratha: Calories 39 • Protein 1g • Carbohydrates 5g • Fat 1.6g

Stuffed Bajra Roti

Preparation time: 10 minutes ● Cooking time: 30 minutes ● Makes 8 rotis.

For the dough
2 teacups bajra flour
a pinch salt

To be mixed into a stuffing
½ teacup crumbled paneer, *page 135*
2 tablespoons chopped fenugreek
(methi) leaves
1 chopped green chilli
1 finely chopped large tomato
salt to taste

For serving
2 teaspoons butter (optional)

For the dough
1. Add salt and hot water to the bajra
   flour and make a dough.
2. Knead well, divide into 16 portions
   and roll out each portion into thin
   rotis.

How to proceed
1. Spread a little stuffing on one roti.
   Then put another roti on top and
   press well so that it becomes one roti.
   Repeat for the remaining rotis and
   stuffing.
2. Cook each stuffed roti on a tawa
   (griddle) on both sides without oil.

★ Serve hot. If you like, apply a little
butter, before serving.

Health Information: Bajra is a coarse millet which has no gluten and can be eaten
by people requiring gluten-free diets. This roti is high in fibre and iron.

Per Roti: Calories 115 ● Protein 7g ● Carbohydrates 18g ● Fat 1.4g

Minty Stuffed Parathas

Preparation time: 30 minutes ● Cooking time: 45 minutes ● Makes 20 parathas.

For the dough
2   teacups whole wheat flour
½ teaspoon salt
2   teaspoons oil

For the mint sauce (for the dough)
¾ teacup mint leaves
1   teaspoon lemon juice
½ level teaspoon cumin seeds
3   green chillies
1   level teaspoon salt

For the stuffing
2   teacups chopped cabbage
1   teacup boiled green peas
1   chopped potato
1   chopped onion
juice of 1 lemon
2   pinches garam masala
1   tablespoon chopped coriander
1   tablespoon ground green chilli
½ level teaspoon sugar
2   teaspoons oil
salt to taste

For cooking
2   teaspoons oil *or* butter

For the dough
1. Pour all the ingredients for the sauce with ½ teacup of water into a mixer and blend.
2. Mix the mint sauce with the wheat flour, oil and salt and prepare a soft dough.
3. Knead well and divide into 20 portions. Roll out the portions into thin rotis.

For the stuffing
1. Sprinkle salt over the cabbage and leave aside for 10 minutes. Thereafter, squeeze out the water from the cabbage using your hands.
2. Crush the green peas.
3. Heat the oil and add the potato and crushed peas. Sprinkle a little water on top, cover and cook until soft.
4. Add the cabbage and onion and cook for 1 minute.
5. Add the lemon juice, garam masala, coriander, green chilli, sugar and salt.
6. Divide into 20 portions.

continued ...

Accompaniment

1½ teacups fresh curds, *page 134,*
   (optional)

How to proceed

1. Put one portion of the stuffing on each roti and fold.
2. Arrange all the stuffed rotis in a greased baking tray.
3. Brush lightly with a little ghee or butter and bake in a hot oven at 200°C until pink spots appear. Alternatively, cook on a tawa (griddle) on both sides and brush lightly with oil or butter.

★ Serve hot with fresh curds.

Note: 1½ teacups curds contain 93.5 calories i.e. 5 calories per serving.

Health Information: A high fibre paratha having complex carbohydrates which are a better kind of energy supply than the simple carbohydrates obtained from pure sugar. An excellent recipe for athletes who need complex carbohydrates and a little fat.

Per Paratha: Calories 91 ● Protein 3g ● Carbohydrates 17g ● Fat 1.4g

Paneer Palak Methi Rotis

PICTURE ON PAGE 36

Preparation time: 10 minutes ● Cooking time: 15 minutes ● Makes 6 rotis.

For the dough
1 teacup whole wheat flour
1 teaspoon oil
½ teacup finely chopped fenugreek
  (methi) leaves and palak
1 tablespoon fresh curds, *page 134*
½ teaspoon chilli powder
¼ teaspoon turmeric powder
a pinch asafoetida
½ teaspoon sugar
salt to taste

For the topping
½ teacup finely chopped fenugreek
  (methi) leaves and palak
1 tablespoon grated paneer, *page 135*

For the dough
1. Mix the ingredients and knead into a
   dough. Add more curds if required to
   make the dough.
2. Divide into 6 portions and roll out
   into rotis.
3. Cook on a tawa (griddle) on both
   sides.

How to proceed
When you want to serve, sprinkle a
little topping on top of each roti. Place
below the grill for 1 minute.

* Serve hot.

Health Information: Methi, palak and paneer, when added to the whole wheat
chapati increase the calcium content more than 7 times. Methi is rich in calcium
and Vitamins A and C.

Per Roti: Calories 90 ● Protein 4g ● Carbohydrates 16g ● Fat 1.4g

Rice and Moong Dal Idli

Preparation time: 20 minutes ● Cooking time: 30 minutes ● Serves 8.

½ teacup rice
½ teacup moong dal
¼ teaspoon fenugreek (methi) seeds
(optional)
a pinch soda bi-carb
salt to taste

1. Soak the rice, dal and fenugreek seeds in water for 5 to 6 hours.
2. Grind the soaked ingredients in a mixer and leave the batter aside for at least 8 hours or preferably overnight.
3. Thereafter, add the soda bi-carb and salt and pour a little mixture into the cavities of a small idli maker.
4. Steam in a cooker for a few minutes. Repeat for the remaining mixture.

★ Serve hot with chutney.

Health Information: This novel combination gives idlis having a different flavour and a higher protein content.

Per Serving: Calories 66 ● Protein 3g ● Carbohydrates 13g ● Fat 0.4g

Suji Idli

PICTURE ON PAGE 54

Preparation time: 10 minutes ● Cooking time: 25 minutes ● Makes 70 small idlis.

1 teacup semolina (suji)
1 teacup fresh curds, *page 134*
1 teaspoon fruit salt
1 teacup finely chopped cabbage
1 chopped onion
2 tablespoons chopped coriander
a few curry leaves
2 to 3 finely chopped green chillies
salt to taste

1. Roast the semolina on a tawa (griddle) without any oil until it becomes yellow or very light pink in colour.
2. Mix the curds with the fruit salt and add the remaining ingredients to make a batter.
3. Steam in a small idli mould for 10 minutes.

★ Serve hot.

Health Information: Small finger snacks which are low in calories. Rich in Vitamins K, C and essential amino acids.

Per Idli: Calories 8 ● Protein 0.5g ● Carbohydrates 2g ● Fat 0g

Moong Dal Dhoklas

PICTURE ON PAGE 36

Preparation time: 20 minutes • Cooking time: 20 minutes • Makes 16 pieces.

1 teacup moong dal with skin
2 teaspoon gram flour (besan)
2 green chillies
1 tablespoon fresh curds, *page 134*
2 teaspoons fruit salt
a pinch asafoetida
salt to taste

For the topping
2 tablespoons finely chopped cabbage
2 tablespoons finely chopped carrots

1. Soak the moong dal for 2 hours. Drain.
2. Add the green chillies and a little water and grind in a mixer.
3. Add the gram flour, curds, asafoetida and salt.
4. When you want to serve, add the fruit salt and mix well.
5. Pour the mixture into two thalis of about 200 mm. diameter. Sprinkle the cabbage on top and steam for 5 minutes.

★ Serve hot.

Health Information: A protein-rich Gujarati speciality without oil. Excellent with meals or for breakfast or tea-time.

Per Serving: Calories 36 • Protein 3g • Carbohydrates 6g • Fat 0.4g

Spicy Spinach Dumplings

PICTURE ON PAGE 117

Preparation time: 10 minutes ● Cooking time: 10 minutes ● Makes 10 pieces.

2 teacups finely chopped spinach
1 chopped green chilli
1 tablespoon gram flour (besan)
2 teaspoons whole wheat flour
2 teaspoons fresh curds, *page 134*,
  (optional)
a pinch asafoetida
a pinch sugar
1 teaspoon oil
salt to taste

1. Mix all the ingredients, using curds if the mixture is too dry for shaping.
2. Shape into small flat rounds.
3. Steam the rounds in a cooker for 5 to 7 minutes.

★ Serve hot.

Health Information: A light, vitamin-rich snack for spinach lovers made using the calorie reducing steaming technique.

Per Piece: Calories 17 ● Protein 1g ● Carbohydrates 2g ● Fat 0.6g

Moong Dal Dahi Wadas

Preparation time: 15 minutes • Cooking time: 15 minutes • Makes 8 wadas.

½ teacup moong dal (with skin)
2 green chillies
a pinch asafoetida
½ teaspoon soda bi-carb *or* fruit salt
2 teacups fresh curds, *page 134*
2 pinches roasted cumin powder
2 pinches chilli powder
1 tablespoon chopped coriander (optional)
salt to taste

For the seasoning
½ teaspoon mustard seeds
3 to 4 pieces green chillies
a pinch asafoetida
1½ teaspoons oil

1. Soak the moong dal for 3 to 4 hours. Drain.
2. Add the green chillies and blend in a mixer with very little water.
3. Add the asafoetida and soda bi-carb and mix well.
4. Heat a non-stick sandwich toaster and spread 1 teaspoon of the mixture in each cavity. Close and heat. When ready, the mixture will be toasted into pieces of triangular shape. Take out the toasts.
5. Dip the toasts in water for 5 minutes. Thereafter, squeeze out the water and arrange the wadas on a plate.
6. Beat the curds with the salt.
7. To prepare the seasoning, heat the oil and fry the mustard seeds for ½ minute. Add the green chillies and asafoetida. Mix the seasoning with the beaten curds.

★ Spread the seasoned curds over the wadas. Sprinkle the cumin powder, chilli powder and coriander on top and serve. If you like, also sprinkle sweet and sour chutney, *page 132*.

Health Information: Instead of the traditional method of frying dahi wadas, this recipe uses a different cooking technique to give a healthier dish which is lower in calories and fat.

Per Wada: Calories 61 • Protein 4.5g • Carbohydrates 7.5g • Fat 1.6g

Moong Dal Panki

Preparation time: 10 minutes ● Cooking time: 10 minutes ● Makes 8 pankies.

50 grams moong dal
1 tablespoon fresh curds, *page 134*
2 green chillies
1 teaspoon gram flour (besan)
a pinch asafoetida
1 tablespoon chopped coriander
a pinch sugar
½ teaspoon lemon juice
salt to taste

1. Soak the moong dal in water for 2 hours. Drain.
2. Grind with the fresh curds and green chillies.
3. Add the gram flour, asafoetida, coriander, sugar, lemon juice and salt and mix well.
4. Grease balana leaves lightly.
5. Spread 1 tablespoon of the mixture on one leaf and cover with another leaf. Roast on a tawa (griddle) until brown spots appear on both sides.

★ Serve hot with green chutney, *page 129*

Health Information: An excellent low calorie snack which is a good source of protein.

Per Panki: Calories 28 ● Protein 2g ● Carbohydrates 5g ● Fat 0.3g

Masoor Dal with Rice

Preparation time: 10 minutes ● Cooking time: 40 minutes ● Serves 4.

100 grams uncooked rice
½ teacup uncooked masoor *or* tur dal
1 teaspoon cumin seeds
2 slit green chillies
100 grams cauliflower pieces
2 tablespoons diced carrots
¼ teaspoon turmeric powder
1 sliced tomato
1 tablespoon chopped coriander
2 teaspoons ghee
salt to taste

1. Cook the rice. Cool and keep aside.
2. Cook the dal in a pressure cooker. Add 2½ teacups of water to the cooked dal and beat well.
3. Heat the ghee and fry the cumin seeds for a while.
4. Add the onion slices and green chillies and cook for a while.
5. Add the cooked dal, cauliflower, carrots, turmeric and salt and cook for 10 minutes on a slow flame.
6. Finally, add the tomato and chopped coriander and cook for a few minutes.

★ Serve the dal with the cooked rice.

Health Information: The protein contained in rice and dal complement each other to give a higher quality protein which is the corner stone of our nutritious meal. Be sure not to rinse the rice more than required to remove the dirt since excess washing will result in loss of vitamins.

Per Serving: Calories 188 ● Protein 7g ● Carbohydrates 34g ● Fat 3.5g

Moong Misal

Preparation time: 10 minutes ● Cooking time: 5 minutes ● Serves 6.

1 teacup sprouted moong, *page 131*
1 teacup fresh curds, *page 134*
4 teaspoons sweet and sour chutney, *page 132*
2 chopped tomatoes
2 chopped onions
a little cumin seed powder
2 teaspoons oil
salt and chilli powder to taste

1. Heat the oil, add the moong, ½ teacup of water and salt. Cover and cook on a low flame until the moong is soft.
2. Beat the curds with a pinch of salt.

How to serve
Spread the hot moong on a serving plate. Top with the beaten curds, the chutney, tomatoes, onions, cumin seed powder, chilli powder and salt.

★ Serve immediately.

Health Information: The recipe combines the proteins of moong beans and a dairy product so as to make the proteins complete.

Per Serving: Calories 87 ● Protein 5g ● Carbohydrates 12.5g ● Fat 2.1g

WESTERN BREAKFAST
1. PAPAYA BALLS, 75 grams
2. CARROT AND PANEER TOAST, two toast, page 121
3. BLACK GRAPES, 75 grams
4. HOT TEA WITH LEMON, one cup

Health information: Begin your day with this healthy breakfast which is rich in essential amino acids, fibre and many vitamins and minerals

Per Breakfast: Calories 343 ● Protein 18g ● Carbohydrates 63g ● Fat 4.8g

Pumpkin Handva

Preparation time: 10 minutes • Cooking time: 15 minutes • Serves 5.

3 teacups grated white pumpkin (lauki)
5 tablespoons coarse jowar flour
1 chopped green chilli
2 tablespoons chopped coriander
¼ teaspoon soda bi-carb
2 pinches sugar
salt to taste

For the topping
1 chopped tomato
1 chopped onion
2 tablespoons tomato ketchup *or* sweet
   and sour sauce, *page 131*

1. Squeeze out a little water from the pumpkin. Add the flour, green chilli, coriander, soda bi-carb, sugar and salt and mix well.
2. Spread the mixture on a baking tray and bake in a hot oven at 225° C for 15 minutes. Top with the tomato, onion and ketchup or sweet and sour sauce.

★ Cut into pieces and serve.

Health Information: Pumpkin contains 96% water and makes this traditional Gujarati dish low in calories. Jowar contains more iron than wheat flour. It also imparts an unusual flavour to the handva.

Per Serving: Calories 79 • Protein 2g • Carbohydrates 17g • Fat 0.5g

WESTERN LUNCH
1. LENTIL SOUP, one cup, page 24
2. WHOLE WHEAT BURGER, one, page 114
3. BEAN SPROUTS SALAD, one serving, page 39

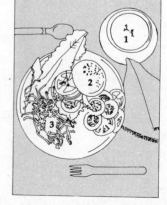

Health information: Beans and curds make this meal very rich in essential amino acids and complex carbohydrates. This lunch is very filling due to the high fibre burger and beans.

Per Lunch: Calories 333 • Protein 16g • Carbohydrates 59g • Fat 6g

Cauliflower with Chutney

Preparation time: 15 minutes • Cooking time: 15 minutes • Serves 6 to 8.

2 medium sized cauliflower
1 tablespoon crumbled paneer, *page 135*, for baking

To be ground into a chutney paste
1 teacup chopped coriander
4 green chillies
2 tablespoons grated fresh coconut
1 teaspoon sugar
½ teaspoon salt
1 teaspoon lemon juice

For the sauce
2 fresh tomatoes
1 grated onion
½ teaspoon chilli powder
2 tablespoons tomato ketchup
1 teaspoon sugar
4 teaspoons oil
salt to taste

1. Steam the cauliflower in salted water.
2. Stuff the cauliflower with the paste.

For the sauce
1. Put the tomatoes in hot water. After 10 minutes, grate them.
2. Heat the oil and fry the onion for 2 minutes.
3. Add the remaining ingredients and cook again for 2 minutes.

How to proceed
1. Pour the sauce over the stuffed cauliflower.
2. Sprinkle with the paneer and bake in a hot oven at 200°C for 10 to 15 minutes.

★ Serve hot.

Health Information: Cauliflower and coriander are sources of the highest amounts of Vitamin C amongst vegetables. The chutney is rich in iron and calcium. The cauliflower is steamed to minimize the loss of Vitamin C.

Per Serving: Calories 92 • Protein 4g • Carbohydrates 11g • Fat 4.3g

Spicy Tomato Rasam

Preparation time: 5 minutes ● Cooking time: 25 minutes ● Makes 12 cups.

For the masala powder
1 teaspoon cumin seeds
1½ teaspoons coriander seeds
8 peppercorns

Other ingredients
1 kg. tomatoes
3 tablespoons tamarind water
1 teaspoon lemon juice
2 pinches turmeric powder
½ teaspoon chilli powder
¼ teaspoon asafoetida
salt to taste

For garnish
1 tablespoon chopped coriander

For the masala powder
Roast the cumin seeds, coriander seeds and peppercorns for 1 minute. Grind into a masala powder.

How to proceed
1. Cut the tomatoes in half and place in 8 glasses of boiling water.
2. Add the remaining ingredients including the masala powder and boil for a further 10 minutes.
3. Break the tomatoes with a spoon.
4. Boil again for 10 minutes.

★ Garnish with chopped coriander and serve hot.

Health Information: In this South Indian recipe, the spices help to increase flavour and decrease salt requirement. Tomatoes provide a lot of Vitamins A, C, and K.

Per Cup: Calories 25 ● Protein 1g ● Carbohydrates 5g ● Fat 0.4g

Mixed Pulses with Vegetables

Preparation time: 20 minutes ● Cooking time: 50 minutes ● Serves 8.

2   tablespoons whole moong
2   tablespoons gram (chana)
1   tablespoon whole masoor
175 grams cauliflower
6   to 7 small whole onions
2   sliced onions
2   large chopped tomatoes
3   teaspoons oil
salt to taste
1   sliced tomato and 1 tablespoon
    chopped coriander for decoration

To be ground into a paste
8   cloves garlic
8   red chillies
2   teaspoons coriander seeds
2   teaspoons cumin seeds
25mm. piece ginger

1. Soak the moong, gram and masoor in water for at least 6 hours. Drain and allow to sprout for 12 hours.
2. Add 2 teacups of water and cook in a pressure cooker.
3. Cut the cauliflower into big pieces and boil with the whole onions.

How to proceed
1. Heat the oil and fry the sliced onions for 3 minutes.
2. Add the paste and fry again for 3 to 4 minutes.
3. Add the soaked pulses and cook for a few minutes.
4. Add the cauliflower, whole onions, tomatoes and salt and cook for at least 10 minutes. If you like, add 3 to 4 teaspoons of tamarind water before serving.

★ Serve hot decorated with tomato slices and chopped coriander.

Health Information: This combination of pulses and mixed vegetables gives a protein-rich dish.

Per Serving: Calories 88 ● Protein 4g ● Carbohydrates 13g ● Fat 2.6g

6. Western Dishes

Cabbage Rolls

Preparation time: 15 minutes • Cooking time: 30 minutes • Serves 4.

10 to 15 large cabbage leaves
2 teacups finely chopped mixed boiled vegetables (carrots, french beans, cauliflower, green peas)
1 finely chopped onion
2 chopped green chillies
1 teacup tomato gravy, *page 130*
50 grams paneer, *page 135*
1 tablespoon oil
salt and pepper to taste

1. Cook the cabbage leaves in salted water for 1 minute. Drain thoroughly.
2. Heat the oil and fry the onion for a few seconds.
3. Add the green chillies and fry again for a few seconds.
4. Add the vegetables, salt and pepper.
5. Place a little vegetable mixture on each cabbage leaf and spread a little tomato gravy on top.
6. Roll up each leaf and arrange on a greased baking dish.
7. Boil the balance tomato gravy and pour over the rolls. Sprinkle the paneer on top.

★ Serve immediately. If you like, use grated cooking cheese instead of the paneer and bake in a hot oven at 225° C for 10 minutes before serving.

Variation: CABBAGE ROLLS IN WHITE SAUCE Instead of tomato gravy, use 1½ teacups of white sauce, *page 130*, and bake before serving.

Health Information: A recipe which uses a low-calorie vegetable like cabbage and yet gives a Mediterranean flavour. It provides more than half of a teenager's daily requirement of Vitamins A, C and K.

Per Serving: Calories 130 • Protein 7g • Carbohydrates 14g • Fat 5.5g

Baked Paneer in Spinach with Tomato Gravy

Preparation time: 20 minutes ● Cooking time: 30 minutes ● Serves 8.

For the spinach
6 teacups chopped spinach
1 chopped onion
2 teaspoons plain flour
3 chopped green chillies
2 teaspoons oil
salt to taste

Other ingredients
200 grams paneer, *page 135*, chopped
2 teacups chopped mixed boiled
vegetables (french beans, carrots,
cauliflower)
1 teacup tomato gravy, *page 130*
salt to taste

For the spinach
1. Cook the spinach without adding any
   water.
2. When cooked, blend in a liquidiser.
3. Heat the oil and fry the onion for ½
   minute.
4. Add the flour and fry again for ½
   minute.
5. Add the green chillies, spinach and
   salt and cook for 1 minute.

How to proceed
1. Mix the spinach with the paneer,
   vegetables and salt and spread in a
   baking dish.
2. Pour the tomato gravy on top.
3. If you like, grate a little of the paneer
   and sprinkle on top.
4. Bake in a hot oven at 200° C for 10
   minutes.

★ Serve hot.

Health Information: An excellent combination of a dairy product (which provides proteins) with green and starchy vegetables which supply iron, vitamins, minerals and complete carbohydrates.

Per Serving: Calories 108 ● Protein 11g ● Carbohydrates 12g ● Fat 2.5g

Vegetable Florentine

Preparation time: 15 minutes • Cooking time: 35 minutes • Serves 8.

For the spinach
10 teacups finely chopped spinach
1 chopped onion
2 teaspoons plain flour (optional)
2 chopped green chillies
2 teaspoons skim milk powder
a pinch soda bi-carb
2 teaspoons oil
salt and pepper to taste

For the vegetables
2 teacups chopped mixed boiled
   vegetables (french beans, carrots,
   cauliflower, green peas)
2 teacups white sauce, *page 130*
salt and pepper to taste

For baking
2 tablespoons grated cooking cheese

For the spinach
1. Add the soda bi-carb and 2 teaspoons
   of water to the spinach and cook until
   soft.
2. Drain out the liquid and blend the
   solids in a liquidiser.
3. Heat the oil and fry the onion, flour
   and green chillies for ½ minute.
4. Add 3 teaspoons of water to the skim
   milk powder and mix well. Add to
   the onion green chilli mixture.
5. Add the spinach mixture, salt and
   pepper and cook for 1 minute.

For the vegetables
To the white sauce, add the vegetables,
salt and pepper. Mix well.

How to proceed
1. Spread the spinach mixture on a
   greased baking dish and cover with
   the vegetable mixture.
2. Sprinkle the grated cooking cheese
   on top and bake in a hot oven at 225°
   C for about 20 minutes.

★ Serve hot.

Health Information: This filling dish is enriched with spinach which provides iron,
calcium and folic acid.

Per Serving: Calories 101 • Protein 7g • Carbohydrates 13g • Fat 2.5g

Sizzler

PICTURE ON PAGE 89

Preparation time: 15 minutes • Cooking time: 10 minutes • Makes 1 meal.

For the moong
5   tablespoons sprouted moong *or* sprouted math beans, *page 131*
1   chopped onion
1   chopped tomato
½   teaspoon chopped green chilli
2   teaspoons oil
1   teaspoon chopped coriander
salt to taste

For the cutlets
50 grams paneer, *page 135*
½   teacup grated cabbage
½   teacup chopped onion
2   chopped green chillies
1   tablespoon chopped coriander
1   teaspoon oil
salt to taste

Other ingredients
1   teacup boiled cauliflower pieces
1   teacup boiled carrot slices
1   capsicum stuffed with corn filling, *page 92*
1   baked stuffed tomato, *page 87*

For the moong
1. Heat the oil and fry the onion for 1 minute.
2. Add the tomato and green chilli and fry again for ½ minute.
3. Add the moong and sprinkle a little water over the moong. Add salt and cover and cook for 3 to 4 minutes i.e. till partly cooked.

For the cutlets
1. Grate the paneer. Add the cabbage, onion, green chillies, coriander and salt and shape into 2 cutlets.
2. Cook on both sides on a tawa (griddle) which is brushed with very little oil.

How to proceed
1. When you want to serve, heat a sizzler plate in an oven for at least 10 minutes.
2. Arrange the cauliflower, carrot, stuffed capsicum, stuffed tomato, moong and cutlets on the plate.
3. Heat the tray for ½ minute and sprinkle the tomato ketchup mixed with a little water over this to get the sizzling effect.

Health Information: Makes a complete balanced meal containing adequate amounts of all the major food groups. It is very rich in proteins, complex carbohydrates, fibres and also vitamins and many minerals including iron, calcium etc. A healthy variation of the usual sizzler containing fried potato chips and cutlets and very little protein.

For 1 meal: Calories 586 • Protein 36g • Carbohydrates 72g • Fat 19g

Spinach and Paneer in Tomato Gravy

Preparation time: 15 minutes • Cooking time: 15 minutes • Serves 4.

4 teacups spinach leaves
3 tablespoons crumbled paneer, *page 135*
1 finely chopped green chilli
1 teacup tomato gravy, *page 130*
salt to taste

1. Steam the spinach leaves for a few minutes.
2. Chop the steamed spinach.
3. Add the paneer, green chilli and salt.
4. Spread the mixture on a baking dish and pour tomato gravy on top.
5. Bake in a hot oven at 200° C for 10 minutes.

★ Serve hot.

Health Information: A main dish which is unbelievably low in calories and has all the goodness of spinach and paneer.

Per Serving: Calories 67 • Protein 7g • Carbohydrates 7g • Fat 1.8g

Mixed Vegetables in Creamy Sauce

Preparation time: 10 minutes • Cooking time: 15 minutes • Serves 2.

1 teacup sliced and boiled mixed vegetables (french beans, carrots, cauliflower)
1 chopped onion
1 chopped green chilli
1 teacup white sauce, *page 130*
1 teaspoon butter
salt and pepper to taste

1. Heat the butter and fry the onion for ½ minute.
2. Add the green chilli and fry again for ½ minute.
3. Add the vegetables and cook for 1 minute.
4. Add the white sauce, salt and pepper and mix thoroughly.

★ Serve hot.

Health Information: A dish which sounds and tastes rich and creamy but uses the unusual low calorie white sauce.

Per Serving: Calories 113 • Protein 5g • Carbohydrates 16g • Fat 4g

Baked Canneloni

PICTURE ON PAGE 108

Preparation time: 20 minutes • Cooking time: 30 minutes • Serves 8.

For the dough
1 teacup whole wheat flour
2 teaspoons oil
salt to taste

For the stuffing
2 teacups finely chopped mixed boiled
  vegetables (french beans, carrots,
  cauliflower, green peas)
50 grams paneer, *page 135*
1 chopped onion
1 teaspoon chilli powder
2 teaspoons oil
salt to taste

For the sauce
1 teacup tomato gravy, *page 130*

For the topping
2 tablespoons grated paneer, *page 135*

For the dough
1. Mix the flour, oil and salt. Add water
   and prepare a soft dough.
2. Keep the dough aside for 1 hour.

For the stuffing
1. Heat the oil and fry the onion for ½
   minute.
2. Add the remaining ingredients and
   cook for 1 minute.

How to proceed
1. Roll out the dough into small thin
   rounds of 100 to 125 mm. diameter.
2. Boil the water in a vessel and add 1
   tablespoon of oil.
3. Drop one round of dough at a time
   into the boiling water, cook for ½
   minute and remove.
4. Repeat for the remaining rounds.
5. Fill each round with 1 tablespoon of
   the stuffing and roll up like a
   pancake.
6. Arrange the canneloni on a greased
   baking dish and pour hot tomato
   gravy on top.
7. Sprinkle the paneer on top.
8. Bake in a hot oven at 200° C for 10
   minutes.

★ Serve hot.

Health Information: A well-balanced main dish with an Italian flavour using
paneer for protein and whole wheat flour and vegetables for minerals, vitamins
and fibre.

Per Serving: Calories 113 • Protein 5g • Carbohydrates 16g • Fat 3.5g

Stuffed Cabbage Leaves with Spinach

Preparation time: 10 minutes • Cooking time: 20 minutes • Makes 12 pieces.

6   cabbage leaves
1   chopped onion
1   chopped green chilli
4   teacups finely chopped spinach
2   tablespoons paneer, *page 135*
2   teacups white sauce, *page 130*
2   ·teaspoons oil
salt to taste

1. Put the cabbage leaves in boiling water for 5 minutes. Remove the thick stems.
2. Drain and cut each cabbage leaf into 2 pieces.
3. Heat the oil and fry the onion for ½ minute. Add the green chilli and fry again for a few seconds. Add the spinach and cook for 1 minute. Drain the water if any. Add the paneer and salt and mix well.
4. Fill the cabbage leaves with this mixture. Spread a little white sauce inside. Make packets or rolls of each leaf and close.
5. Arrange the cabbage in a greased baking dish. Pour the white sauce on top and sprinkle the paneer.
6. Bake in a hot oven at 200°C for 10 minutes.

★ Serve hot.

Health Information: A nutritious and unusual combination of spinach and cabbage containing adequate amounts of many nutrients like calcium, Vitamin C and fibre.

Per Serving: Calories 37 • Protein 2g • Carbohydrates 4g • Fat 1.4g

Stuffed Spinach Leaves in White Sauce

Preparation time: 15 minutes • Cooking time: 15 minutes • Serves 4.

15 to 20 spinach leaves
1 teacup white sauce, *page 130*
1 tablespoon grated paneer, *page 135*

For the stuffing
2 teacups finely chopped mixed boiled
  vegetables (carrots, cauliflower,
  french beans)
1 tablespoon chopped onion
½ teaspoon chopped green chilli
2 teaspoons oil
salt to taste

Put the spinach leaves in salted hot water. After 10 minutes, remove from water.

For the stuffing
1. Heat the oil and fry the onion for ½ minute.
2. Add the green chillies and fry again for a few seconds.
3. Add the vegetables and salt and cook for 1 minute.

How to proceed
1. Fill the spinach leaves with the stuffing and put them on a well greased baking dish.
2. Spread the white sauce and paneer on top.
3. Bake in a hot oven at 200°C for 10 to 15 minutes.

★ Serve hot.

Health Information: Combining green leafy vegetables like spinach with mixed vegetables and dairy products gives a well balanced main dish. Take care however to use just enough water whilst boiling the vegetables and to cook them till just tender. In this manner, the loss of Vitamin C during cooking is minimised. Spinach is a good source of iron and vitamins whilst white sauce using cauliflower adds vitamins and reduces calories.

Per Serving: Calories 89 • Protein 4g • Carbohydrates 9g • Fat 4g

Whole Wheat Pasta with Tomato Gravy

Preparation time: 15 minutes • Cooking time: 10 minutes • Serves 2.

For the pasta
100 grams whole wheat flour
2 teaspoons oil
½ teaspoon salt

For serving
½ recipe tomato gravy, *page 130*

For the pasta
1. Mix all the ingredients together and make a stiff dough by adding water. Knead very well and then keep aside for ½ hour.
2. Divide the dough into 2 parts and roll out very thinly. Cut into long strips using a noodle cutter or with a sharp knife.
3. Boil plenty of water in a large vessel and add 1 teaspoon of oil. Put some noodles into the boiling water and cook for 1 minute. Remove the cooked noodles with a sieve and repeat for the remaining noodles. Drain the cooked noodles.

How to serve
Arrange the boiled noodles on individual serving plates and pour the gravy on top.

★ Serve hot.

Health Information: The Italian diet known for its pasta dishes is very well balanced because a typical daily ration of bread and pasta supplies ample complex carbohydrates and protein. And the tomato gravy supplies Vitamin C.

Per Serving: Calories 240 • Protein 7g • Carbohydrates 38g • Fat 7.2g

Indian Vegetable Barbeque

Preparation time: 10 minutes ● Cooking time: 10 minutes ● Serves 2.

For marinating
1 teacup fresh curds, *page 134*
3 teaspoons tandoori masala powder
1½ teaspoons ginger-garlic paste
a few drops red colouring (optional)
salt to taste

Other ingredients
100 grams paneer, *page 135*
2 capsicums
2 tomatoes
2 onions

To serve
1 teaspoon chaat masala (optional)

For marinating
1. Tie the curds in a cloth, hang and allow to drain for 1 hour.
2. Add the masala, paste, colouring and salt and mix well.

How to proceed
1. Cut the paneer into fat squares and capsicum into pieces.
2. Cut the tomatoes and onions in thick circles.
3. Pour the marinate on top of the paneer, capsicum and onion pieces and keep for 20 minutes.

How to serve
1. Just before serving, add the tomato pieces.
2. Now insert one paneer square followed by one capsicum, tomato and onion piece at a time onto 2 skewers.
3. Repeat till the skewer is filled with vegetables.
4. Cook on an open charcoal fire (segree) for 4 to 5 minutes.

★ Sprinkle chaat masala on top and serve hot.

Variation: WESTERN STYLE BARBEQUE
1. Instead of using the marinate, sprinkle salt and ajwain powder on the vegetables.
2. Leave for 5 minutes and then put the vegetables on the skewer.
3. Cook on an open charcoal fire (segree).

★ Serve with mustard, Tabasco sauce and tomato ketchup.

continued ...

Health Information: Marinating the vegetables increases the flavour and makes them more tender. Barbequing is an excellent method of cooking as it avoids the use of oil and imparts a distinctive flavour to the vegetables.

Per Serving: Calories 183 ● Protein 21g ● Carbohydrates 22g ● Fat 1.6g

Baked Stuffed Tomatoes

Preparation time: 10 minutes ● Cooking time: 25 minutes ● Serves 12.

12 medium tomatoes
150 grams crumbled paneer, *page 135*
2 teacups chopped mixed boiled
  vegetables (french beans, carrots,
  cauliflower, green peas)
1 chopped onion
2 chopped green chillies
2 teaspoons oil
salt to taste

1. Cut out the tops of the tomatoes and scoop out the centres. Keep aside the scooped portion.
2. Heat the oil and fry the onion for 1 minute.
3. Add the green chillies and fry again for ½ minute.
4. Add the vegetables, paneer, salt and scooped tomato portion and cook for 2 minutes.
5. Fill the tomatoes with the mixture and bake in a hot oven at 200°C for 20 minutes.

★ Serve hot.

Health Information: A colourful and nutritious dish which is rich in vitamins, amino acids and fibre.

Per Serving: Calories 58 ● Protein 5g ● Carbohydrates 7g ● Fat 1.2g

Baked Tomato Slices

Preparation time: a few minutes ● Cooking time: 10 minutes ● Serves 4.

4 sliced tomatoes
1 teacup white sauce, *page 130*
2 teaspoons grated paneer, *page 135*
salt and pepper to taste

1. Arrange the tomato slices in a baking dish and sprinkle salt and pepper on top.
2. Spread the white sauce over it and sprinkle grated paneer on top.
3. Bake in a hot oven at 200°C for 10 minutes.

★ Serve hot.

Health Information: A light, healthy dish which is simple to prepare. Ideal for lunch.

Per Serving: Calories 39 ● Protein 2g ● Carbohydrates 6g ● Fat 0.8g

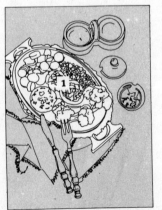

1. SIZZLER, page 80

Tomato Cups with Cottage Cheese

Preparation time: 15 minutes ● No cooking ● Serves 8.

8   medium sized tomatoes
1   teacup paneer, *page 135*
½   teaspoon chopped green chilli
1   teacup finely grated cabbage
1   teacup fresh curds, *page 134*
salt to taste
cucumber slices for garnishing

1. Cut out the tops of the tomatoes and scoop out the centres.
2. Sprinkle a little salt on the cabbage and keep aside for 10 minutes. Then, squeeze out the water.
3. Mix the paneer, green chilli, cabbage, curds and salt.
4. Fill the tomatoes with this mixture. If you like, garnish with cucumber slices.

★ Serve cold on a bed of lettuce.

Health Information: A healthy protein-rich side dish.

Per Serving: Calories 70 ● Protein 10g ● Carbohydrates 7g ● Fat 0.5g

COLD WESTERN LUNCH
1. GAZPACHO, one cup, page 29
2. RUSSIAN SANDWICH, two pieces, page 123
3. LETTUCE CUPS, one serving, page 111

Health information: Makes a light and refreshing summer lunch which is very low in fats. Eating uncooked foods has the advantage that both bulk and nutrient content are preserved.

Per Lunch: Calories 275 ● Protein 14g ● Carbohydrates 51g ● Fat 2.4g

Corn Stuffed Potato

Preparation time: 10 minutes • Cooking time: 50 minutes • Serves 6.

6 large potatoes

For the corn filling
1 teacup cooked corn
1 small onion, finely chopped
1 finely chopped green chilli
1 chopped tomato
2 teaspoons butter
salt and pepper to taste

For the potatoes
1. Brush the potatoes with oil.
2. Wrap in aluminium foil and bake in a hot oven at 200°C till tender (about 30 minutes).
3. Cool and split horizontally.
4. Scoop the potato halves a little so that a slight depression is formed for the filling.

For the corn filling
1. Heat the butter and fry the onion for ½ minute.
2. Add the green chilli and fry again for a few seconds.
3. Add the corn, tomato, salt and pepper and cook for 1 minute.

How to proceed
1. Fill each potato half with the filling (the quantities of the filling are given for six potatoes and should be adjusted as required).
2. Grill under an oven before serving. Alternatively, bake in a hot oven at 200°C for 10 minutes.

★ Serve hot.

Variation: POTATO STUFFED WITH CURD CHEESE DIP Use 1½ recipes of curd cheese dip, *page 43*, in place of the corn stuffing and proceed in same way.

Health Information: Potatoes are wrongly thought of as being fattening. Actually, besides being high in fibre, potatoes are rich in many vitamins, minerals and complex carbohydrates. They should be baked or boiled to make a nutritious and filling meal. It is only when they are fried however (as in the case of french fries) that the calorie content goes up substantially upto as much as three times.

Per Serving: Calories 136 • Protein 3g • Carbohydrates 29g • Fat 1.5g

Tomatoes Stuffed with Bean Sprouts

Preparation time: 5 minutes ● Cooking time: 15 minutes ● Serves 4.

4 medium tomatoes
1½ teacups bean sprouts, *page 136*
2 tablespoons chopped spring onions
½ teaspoon finely chopped green chilli
1 teacup shredded cabbage
2 teaspoons oil
salt to taste

1. Cut the tops of the tomatoes. Scoop out the centres and chop them. Drain the shells.
2. Heat the oil, add the sprouts and spring onions and cook for 2 to 3 minutes. Add the chopped tomato (from centres), green chilli, cabbage and salt and cook for 1 minute.
3. Fill the tomato shells with this mixture.
4. Bake in a hot oven at 200° C for 10 minutes.

★ Serve hot.

Health Information: A protein-rich recipe with vitamins and minerals.

Per Serving: Calories 98 ● Protein 5g ● Carbohydrates 14g ● Fat 3g

Chinese Stir Fried Vegetables

PICTURE ON PAGE 107

Preparation time: 30 minutes ● Cooking time: 10 minutes ● Makes 1 meal.

1   sliced onion
2   chopped spring onions
1   teacup shredded cabbage
½   sliced capsicum
1   sliced tomato
2   tablespoons coarsely grated carrots
2   tablespoons bean sprouts, *page 136*
a pinch baking powder
a pinch citric acid
2   teaspoons soya sauce
2   teaspoons ginger water
1   teaspoon chilli garlic paste
2   teaspoons chillies in vinegar
1   tablespoon oil
salt to taste

To serve
2   bread slices

Heat the oil on a large tawa (griddle) on a high flame. Add the onions, vegetables, baking powder and citric acid and stir for a while. Add the soya sauce, ginger water, chilli garlic paste, chillies in vinegar and salt and mix well.

★ Serve hot with bread slices.

For the ginger water
Grate 12 mm. piece of ginger, add ¼ teacup of water and keep aside for ½ hour.

For the chilli garlic paste
Grind 5 to 6 garlic cloves with 5 red chillies and ¼ teacup of water.

For the chillies in vinegar
Cut 3 to 4 green chillies and add to ½ teacup of white vinegar.

Health Information: A complete, nutritionally balanced meal which is rich in all the food groups. Stir-frying is a nutrient saving technique. Being very fast, it does not introduce as much fat as ordinary frying does and is therefore a superior cooking technique.

Per Meal: Calories 388 ● Protein 11g ● Carbohydrates 48g ● Fat 15g

7. Desserts

Strawberry Yoghurt

Preparation time: a few minutes ● No cooking ● Makes 2 cups.

2 tablespoons strawberry slices
1½ teacups fresh curds, *page 134*
3 teaspoons sugar
1 tablespoon fresh cream, *page 126*

1. Mash the strawberries.
2. Beat the curds with the sugar.
3. Add to the strawberries and mix well.
4. Add the cream.
5. Chill.

Note: To avoid the curds turning sour, prepare 2 hours before use.

Variation: PEACH YOGHURT, picture on *page 108*. Instead of strawberry purée, use 2 tablespoons of finely chopped stewed peaches.

Health Information: A great low-calorie substitute for rich puddings and soufflés, this yoghurt tastes simply delicious.

Per Serving: Calories 78 ● Protein 7g ● Carbohydrates 12g ● Fat 0.7g

Hawaiian Fruit Bowl

Preparation time: 10 minutes ● No cooking ● Serves 6.

1 small pineapple
1 large melon
3 ripe bananas
1 teacup strawberries
2 lemon slices for decoration

Accompaniment

1 teacup vanilla cream, *page 125, or* fresh cream, *page 126*

1. Peel and cut the pineapple and melon into 6 large pieces each.
2. Peel, cut and quarter the bananas. Brush with lemon juice.
3. Pile the strawberries in the centre of a bowl.
4. Arrange the remaining fruit around them.

★ Serve with vanilla cream.

Note: 1 teacup vanilla cream contains 79 calories i.e. 13 calories per serving.

Health Information: A refreshing dessert with all the goodness of fresh fruits. They provide vitamins and minerals as well as fruit sugar which is better for health than table sugar.

Per Serving: Calories 82 ● Protein 1g ● Carbohydrates 20g ● Fat 0.2g

Apple Slices with Vanilla Cream

Preparation time: 5 minutes • Cooking time: 10 minutes • Serves 6.

4 apples
1½ teacups vanilla cream, *page 125*

1. Core out the centres of the apples and then cut into round slices.
2. Steàm the apple slices until soft.
3. Arrange the apple slices on a plate and pour the vanilla cream on top. Place in the refrigerator.

★ Serve cold.

Health Information: A tasty pudding which is easy to make and nutritious too. The high fibre apples will fill you up.

Per Serving: Calories 74 • Protein 2g • Carbohydrates 17g • Fat 0.3g

---

Papaya Pudding

Preparation time: 5 minutes • No cooking • Serves 4.

2 teacups papaya slices
2 tablespoons skim milk, *page 132*
1 teaspoon sugar

1. Blend the papaya, milk and sugar in a liquidiser.
2. Pour the mixture into cups and put to chill.

★ Serve chilled.

Health Information: A light, lunch-time sweet which is unbelievably low in calories. Not only are papayas extremely rich in Vitamin A but they are also easily digestible. This pudding can accordingly be eaten by invalids and children.

Per Serving: Calories 26 • Protein 0.5g • Carbohydrates 6g • Fat 0g

Saffron Cardamom Squares

Preparation time: 5 minutes • Cooking time: 10 minutes • Serves 6.

8 teaspoons chopped China grass
3 teacups skim milk, *page 132*, mixed with 3 teaspoons skim milk powder
3 teaspoons sugar
2 pinches cardamom powder
2 pinches saffron

1. Add 1 teacup of water to the China grass and cook on a slow flame until it dissolves completely. Strain.
2. Boil the milk (keeping aside a little) and add the China grass, sugar and cardamom.
3. Warm the saffron, add the skim milk kept aside and mix until the saffron dissolves.
4. Add to the mixture and heat for 3 to 4 minutes.
5. Spread in a plate and put to set in the refrigerator.

★ When set, cut into square pieces and serve. Alternatively, set in individual glasses and serve.

Variation 1: SAFFRON CARDAMOM ICE-CREAM
Preparation time: 5 minutes • Cooking time: 10 minutes • Serves 4.
1. Omit the skim milk powder and proceed as per steps 1 to 4.
2. Pour the mixture into an ice tray and put to set in the freezer compartment of a refrigerator.
3. To serve, churn the solid ice-cream in a mixer to make it soft and fluffy.

continued ...

Variation 2: VANILLA SQUARES WITH STRAWBERRY SAUCE picture on
page 118
Omit saffron and cardamom powder and use ½ teaspoon vanilla essence instead.
Prepare the strawberry sauce as under.

For the strawberry sauce
1   teacup fresh strawberry purée
2   teaspoons cornflour
8   teaspoons sugar (approx.)
juice of ½ lemon

For the strawberry sauce
1. Mix the cornflour and sugar in 1 teacup of water and cook while stirring continuously.
2. When the sauce is thick and clear, remove the heat.
3. Add the strawberry purée and lemon juice and mix well.
4. Chill.

Health Information: A novel protein-rich and very light Indian sweet with the flavour of saffron and cardamom.

Per Serving: Calories 48 • Protein 8g • Carbohydrates 4g • Fat 0.08g

Sandesh

Preparation time: 5 minutes • Cooking time: 5 minutes • Serves 4.

100 grams freshly made paneer, *page 135*
2   tablespoons milk
4   teaspoons powdered sugar
a few drops rose *or* kewra essence
    (optional)
silver foil *or* fruit pieces for decoration

1. Blend all the ingredients in a mixer.
2. Spread on a serving plate and decorate with silver foil or fruits.
3. Cool.

★ Cut into decorative pieces and serve.

Health Information: The famous Bengali Sandesh made healthier and with fewer calories using skim milk paneer.

Per Serving: Calories 57 • Protein 8g • Carbohydrates 6g • Fat 0.1g

Apple Roll with Vanilla Cream

Preparation time: 10 minutes • Cooking time: 20 minutes • Serves 4.

For the dough

4 tablespoons whole wheat flour *or* plain flour
1 teaspoon oil
a pinch salt

For the apple mixture

½ recipe apple whip, *page 101*

For serving

4 teaspoons vanilla cream, *page 125*

For the dough

1. Mix the flour, oil and salt. Add water and prepare a soft dough.
2. Knead well, divide into 4 portions and roll out into chapaties.

How to proceed

1. Put a little apple mixture in each chapati and close.
2. Arrange the stuffed chapaties on a greased baking tray. Brush lightly with a little butter and bake in a hot oven at 200°C for 10 minutes.

★ Serve with cold vanilla cream.

Health Information: A variation of apple pie using nutritious and unusual whole wheat flour pastry which provides more minerals and vitamins than refined flour.

Per Serving: Calories 122 • Protein 3.6g • Carbohydrates 24g • Fat 1.8g

Kesari Sweet Curds

Preparation time: 5 minutes • Cooking time: 10 minutes • Serves 4.

2¼ teacups skim milk, *page 132*
2   teaspoons skim milk powder
1½ teaspoons fresh curds, *page 134*
4   teaspoons sugar
2   pinches cardamom powder
2   pinches saffron

1. Add the skim milk powder to the prepared milk and mix well.
2. Cool or heat the milk until lukewarm and add the curds, sugar and cardamom powder.
3. Warm the saffron, add 2 teaspoons of the milk mixture and stir until the saffron dissolves.
4. Add the dissolved saffron to the milk and put to set in a closed cupboard.
5. When set, place in the refrigerator.

★ Serve cold.

Health Information: A healthier way of making the traditional sweet curds by substituting skim milk for whole milk. The skim milk, further thickened by skim milk powder, is set to make a protein-rich yoghurt without the fat. Cardamom and saffron are herbs reputed to aid digestion.

Per Serving: Calories 65 • Protein 5g • Carbohydrates 11g • Fat 0.1g

Apple Whip

Preparation time: 5 minutes • Cooking time: 10 minutes • Serves 8.

4   apples
2   teaspoons sugar
½ teaspoon cinnamon powder
1½ teacups vanilla cream, *page 125*

1. Peel, core and slice the apples.
2. Add the sugar and cook in ¾ teacup of water until soft. Mash.
3. Add the cinnamon powder.

★ Serve hot with cold vanilla cream.

Health Information: Cinnamon gives a special flavour to this dessert which is rich in fibre, essential amino acids, vitamins and carbohydrates.

Per Serving: Calories 61 • Protein 1.4g • Carbohydrates 14g • Fat 0.2g

Fruit Salad

PICTURE ON PAGE 118

Preparation time: 10 minutes • No cooking • Serves 6.

2 medium sized apples with peel, sliced
segments of 2 oranges
2 bananas, diced
4 tablespoons seedless green grapes
1 diced pear *or* 1 teacup diced
  honeydew melon
½ bottle (200 to 250 ml. for full bottle) red
  ginger-ale

1. Mix the fruits in a bowl.
2. Pour the ginger-ale over the fruit.
3. Chill for at least 1 hour.

★ Serve cold.

Health Information: This salad is full of vitamins, minerals and fibre. Apples contribute fibre, bananas provide potassium and high fibre whilst grapes are rich in Vitamin C and oranges in Vitamins A, C and minerals.

Per Serving: Calories 80 • Protein 1g • Carbohydrates 20g • Fat 0.4g

Baked Apple Surprise

Preparation time: 10 minutes • Cooking time: 20 minutes • Serves 4.

2 apples
1 banana
a pinch nutmeg powder
a few drops lemon juice
juice of 1 orange
1 teaspoon sugar

1. Mash the banana. Add the nutmeg, lemon juice and sugar.
2. Peel the apples and divide into two. Scoop out the centres.
3. Fill with the banana mixture.
4. Pour the orange juice on top.
5. Bake in a hot oven at 200°C for 20 minutes or until the apples are soft.

★ Serve hot.

Health Information: A high fibre dessert which is filling and is rich in fruit sugar. Ideal for the cold months.

Per Serving: Calories 68 • Protein 0.5g • Carbohydrates 17g • Fat 0.3g

Stewed Pears with Orange Sauce

PICTURE ON PAGE 118

Preparation time: 5 minutes • Cooking time: 5 minutes • Serves 6.

For the stewed pears
6   medium sized pears
7   teaspoons sugar
1   teaspoon lemon juice
2   cloves

Other ingredients
6   tablespoons orange sauce, *page 106*

For the stewed pears
1. Peel and slice the pears.
2. Mix the sugar, lemon juice, cloves and ¾ teacup of water.
3. Add the pears and cook until soft.
4. Cool.

How to proceed
Put the stewed pears into individual bowls. Top with cold orange sauce and serve immediately.

Health Information: Stewing retains the texture and flavour of the fruit. A dessert which is simple to prepare yet sophisticated.

Per Serving: Calories 75 • Protein 0.5g • Carbohydrates 19g • Fat 0.4g

Apples and Saffron Sauce

Preparation time: 10 minutes • Cooking time: 10 minutes • Serves 4.

4   sliced apples
1   teaspoon lemon juice
7   teaspoons sugar
¼   teaspoon saffron

1. Warm the saffron and rub with a little water until it dissolves.
2. Add the lemon juice, sugar, ¾ teacup of water and the apples and cook until soft.
3. Remove the apples and boil the liquid until thick.
4. Spread the sauce over the apples.

★ Serve hot or cold.

Variation: SANDESH WITH GOLDEN APPLES, picture on *page 54*
In the above recipe, use grated apples instead of sliced apples and spread the apples on a serving tray. Top with 1 recipe Sandesh, *page 99*, made somewhat free flowing using 3 instead of 2 tablespoons of milk. Decorate with saffron dots and serve.

Health Information: Saffron gives a traditional flavour to this sauce which goes well with Indian meals.

Per Serving: Calories 100 • Protein 0.2g • Carbohydrates 26g • Fat 0.4g

Stuffed Apples in Saffron Sauce

Preparation time: 15 minutes ● Cooking time: 10 minutes ● Makes 8 apples.

For the apples
8 small sized apples
7 teaspoons sugar
1 teaspoon lemon juice
¼ teaspoon saffron

For the stuffing
100 grams paneer, *page 135*
4 teaspoons powdered sugar
¾ teaspoon rose water
2 tablespoons chopped mixed fruits
(grapes, oranges, pineapples)

For the apples
1. Peel the apples and core the centres.
2. Warm the saffron and rub with a little water until it dissolves.
3. Add the sugar, lemon juice, 1 teacup of water and the apples and cook until soft.
4. Remove the apples from the syrup and keep aside.
5. Boil the syrup until thick.

For the stuffing
1. Dissolve half the sugar in the rose water.
2. Knead the paneer with the remaining sugar and rose water.
3. Add the fruits and mix well.

How to proceed
1. Stuff the apples with the stuffing.
2. Arrange them on a plate and pour the saffron sauce on top.
3. Cool.

★ Serve cold.

Health Information: Here the final dish resembles a rich Bengali sweet, but uses apples instead of sweet chhanna. Apples are lower in calories and have the natural sugar fructose which is healthier.

Per Serving: Calories 83 ● Protein 4g ● Carbohydrates 17g ● Fat 0.4g

Orange Sauce

Preparation time: 5 minutes ● Cooking time: 5 minutes ● Makes 1½ cups.

3 teaspoons chopped China grass
juice of 3 oranges
a few drops lemon juice
3 teaspoons sugar
a few drops orange essence
a few drops orange colouring

1. Add ½ teacup of water to the China grass and cook on a slow flame until it dissolves completely. Strain.
2. Add the orange juice and boil for 1 minute.
3. Cool until lukewarm and then add the lemon juice and sugar.
4. Pour the mixture into an ice tray and put to set in the freezer compartment of a refrigerator. When partially set, stir for a few seconds.
5. Add the orange essence and colouring.

Health Information: A tangy sauce, rich in Vitamin C which complements stewed fruits and vanilla squares.

Per Cup: Calories 116 ● Protein 2g ● Carbohydrates 29g ● Fat 0.2g

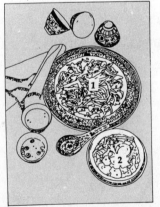

1. CHINESE STIR FRIED VEGETABLES, page 94
2. CHINESE CLEAR VEGETABLE SOUP, page 27

8. Snacks

Mushroom and Tomato Snack

Preparation time: 5 minutes ● Cooking time: 10 minutes ● Serves 8.

200 grams fresh mushrooms
2 medium sized chopped onions
2 medium sized chopped tomatoes
1 chopped green chilli
1 tablespoon chopped coriander
a dash chilli powder (optional)
2 teaspoons oil
4 toasted whole wheat bread slices
salt to taste

1. Heat the oil and fry the onions for ½ minute.
2. Add the tomatoes and fry again for a little while.
3. Add the green chilli, coriander and chilli powder and fry again for ½ minute.
4. Add the mushrooms and salt and cook for a few minutes.

★ Cut each toasted bread slice into two. Spread the mixture on top and serve hot.

Health Information: This wholesome snack uses mushrooms which are good for dieters since they contain 90 per cent water, negligible fat and many vitamins and minerals.

Per Serving: Calories 66 ● Protein 2g ● Carbohydrates 11g ● Fat 1.8g

ITALIAN DINNER
1. GARLIC BREAD, one serving
2. SLIMMERS' SALAD, one serving, page 37
3. PEACH YOGURT, one serving, page 95
4. BOILED CAULIFLOWER, one cup
5. BAKED CANNELONI, one-and-a-half servings, page 82
6. LENTIL AND SPINACH SOUP, one cup, page 26

Health information: You can enjoy a delicious Italian dinner having less than 500 calories. Low calorie paneer and whole wheat flour make nutritious substitute for processed cheese and refined flour. This meal provides all the Vitamins A and C and almost half the proteins, fibre and complex carbohydrates required for the day.

Per Dinner: Calories 480 ● Protein 23g ● Carbohydrates 83g ● Fat 8.4g

Salsa Dip

Preparation time: 15 minutes ● Cooking time: 5 minutes ● Serves 8.

8   tomatoes
2   capsicums
2   finely chopped onions
1   teaspoon chilli powder
2   teaspoons oil
1   teaspoon sugar
salt to taste

Accompaniment
baked puris, *page 116*, (optional)

1. Put the tomatoes in hot water. After 10 minutes, remove the skin and chop.
2. Pierce each capsicum with a fork and hold over the flame until the skin blackens. Remove from the heat, rub off the burnt skin and chop.
3. Heat the oil and fry the onions for ½ minute. Add the tomato, capsicums, chilli powder and salt and cook for a few minutes.

★ This can be served with baked puris.

Note: Each baked puri contains 13 calories.

Health Information: Tomatoes and capsicums are a rich source of Vitamins A and C. Together, they make a wonderful low-calorie sauce for serving with baked corn chips, puris, etc.

Per Serving: Calories 42 ● Protein 1g ● Carbohydrates 6.5g ● Fat 1.6g

Lettuce Cups

PICTURE ON PAGE 90

Preparation time: 15 minutes ● No cooking ● Serves 15.

a few lettuce leaves
2 teacups chopped fruits (apples, pears, watermelon, melon)
1 teacup grated carrots
2 teacups curd cheese dip, *page 43*

1. Place the lettuce leaves and carrots in separate bowls of cold water for about 30 minutes. Drain.
2. Tear the lettuce leaves into small pieces, approximately square in size.
3. Arrange the lettuce pieces in one corner of a large tray, fruits in another and carrots in a third, leaving sufficient margin in the centre.
4. Put the cheese dip in a bowl and place this bowl in the centre of the tray.

★ Let the guests help themselves by putting some fruit on lettuce leaves, some dip as a dressing on top and finally sprinkling grated carrots thereon.

Health Information: The Vitamin A provided by raw carrots is complemented by the proteins from the dressing in this excellent low-calorie cocktail snack.

Per Serving: Calories 16 ● Protein 1g ● Carbohydrates 2.5g ● Fat 0.2g

Mini Pizzas

PICTURE ON PAGE 127

Preparation time: 30 minutes ● Cooking time: 30 minutes ● Makes 16 small pieces.

For the dough
200 grams whole wheat flour
10 grams fresh yeast
¾ teaspoon salt
¾ teaspoon sugar
1 teaspoon oil

For the sauce
400 grams tomatoes
2 small onions, chopped
3 to 4 cloves crushed garlic
½ teaspoon chilli powder
1 teaspoon sugar
½ teaspoon oregano *or* a pinch ajwain
1 teaspoon oil
salt to taste

For the topping
2 capsicums, cut into rings
4 onions, cut into rings
2 tomatoes, cut into slices
50 grams grated paneer, *page 135* or
75 grams mozzarella cheese

For the dough
1. Sieve the flour with the salt and sugar. Add the oil and mix well.
2. Make a well in the centre and crumble the yeast in the centre.
3. Sprinkle ½ teacup of warm water over the yeast. Wait for a few minutes.
4. Mix the yeast in the flour and add enough water to make a dough.
5. Cover the dough with a wet cloth to "prove". Leave for 30 minutes or until it is double in size.
6. Knead the dough for 1 minute.
7. Divide the dough into 16 parts.
8. Roll out each part to 75 to 100mm. diameter rounds.
9. Prick lightly with a fork.
10. Brush a baking tray lightly with oil and arrange the rounds on the tray. Keep aside for 15 minutes.
11. Bake in a hot oven at 200°C for 15 minutes.

continued ...

For the sauce
1. Chop the tomatoes and drain.
2. Heat the oil, add the onions and garlic and fry for 3 minutes.
3. Add the tomatoes, chilli powder, sugar and salt and boil for 10 minutes.
4. Blend the mixture in a liquidiser.
5. Add the oregano.

How to proceed
1. When you want to serve, spread some sauce on top of each pizza.
2. Arrange the capsicum and onion rings and tomato slices on top.
3. Sprinkle the paneer on top. If you like, use a mixture of paneer and cream.
4. Bake in a hot oven at 200°C for 5 to 10 minutes.

★ Cut into pieces and serve hot.

Health Information: Prepared in this way, the pizza provides proteins in the cheese, carbohydrates in the crust and vitamins and minerals in the tomato sauce which shifts it from the level of junk food to that of a health food.

Per Serving: Calories 75 • Protein 3.5g • Carbohydrates 14g • Fat 0.8g

Whole Wheat Burgers

PICTURE ON PAGE 72

Preparation time: 15 minutes • Cooking time: 5 minutes • Makes 6 burgers.

6 brown bread buns, *page 133*
12 tomato slices
12 lettuce leaves
6 onion slices (optional)
2 teaspoons tomato ketchup mixed with
   1 teaspoon chilli sauce (optional)
made mustard to taste
cress for decoration

For the cutlets

3 teacups finely chopped mixed
   vegetables (carrots, cabbage,
   cauliflower, potatoes, french beans)
¼ teaspoon turmeric powder
1 tablespoon whole wheat *or* plain flour
1 tablespoon chopped coriander
1 chopped green chilli
1 tablespoon oil
salt to taste

For the cutlets

1. Heat the oil and add the vegetables,
   turmeric and salt. Cover and cook on
   a slow flame until the vegetables are
   cooked.
2. Sprinkle the flour on the vegetables,
   mix and cook again for a few
   minutes.
3. Mash the vegetables lightly. Add the
   coriander and green chilli, mix well
   and shape into 16 cutlets.
4. Brush a non-stick frying pan lightly
   with oil and cook each cutlet on both
   sides. If you like, you can roll into
   wholemeal bread crumbs before
   cooking.

How to proceed

1. Slice each bun into two.
2. On the cut portion of each bun, apply
   a little mustard, a little tomato
   ketchup and firstly arrange 2 lettuce
   leaves, then one cutlet, one onion
   slice and two tomato slices.

★ Decorate with cress and serve hot.

Health Information: A wholesome high fibre lunch or snack with the goodness of wholewheat bread and fresh vegetables. A healthy "fast food".

Per Burger: Calories 147 • Protein 5g • Carbohydrates 25g • Fat 3.4g

Cucumber Snack

PICTURE ON PAGE 117

Preparation time: a few minutes ● No cooking ● Serves 4.

3 medium cucumbers
50 grams paneer, *page 135*
1 teaspoon freshly chopped dill (suva)
¼ teaspoon chopped green chilli
3 teaspoons fresh curds, *page 134*
salt to taste

1. Divide each cucumber into two, horizontally. Scoop out the centres.
2. Grate the paneer. Add the dill, chilli, curds and salt.
3. Fill the cucumber centres with the paneer mixture. Cut into slices.

★ Decorate with a sprig of dill and serve.

Health Information: A low-calorie snack which is rich in proteins from dairy products and Vitamin C from cucumbers and dill.

Per Serving: Calories 29 ● Protein 4g ● Carbohydrates 2g ● Fat 0.2g

Masala Puri

Preparation time: 5 minutes ● Cooking time: 15 minutes ● Makes 25 puris.

100 grams whole wheat flour
½ teaspoon coarsely powdered cumin seeds
½ teaspoon coarsely powdered peppercorn
¼ teaspoon turmeric powder (optional)
2 teaspoons oil
¼ teaspoon salt

1. Mix all the ingredients. Add water and prepare a stiff dough. Knead well.
2. Divide the dough into 25 portions.
3. Roll out into thin puris and prick with a fork.
4. Arrange the puris on a baking tray.
5. Bake in a hot oven at 200°C for 15 minutes.

Health Information: You need lesser usage of salt because of the flavour imparted by herbs and masalas.

Per Puri: Calories 18 ● Protein 0.5g ● Carbohydrates 3g ● Fat 0.4g

Baked Puri

PICTURE ON PAGE 128

Preparation time: 5 minutes ● Cooking time: 10 minutes ● Makes 25 puris.

100 grams whole wheat flour
1   teaspoon oil
¼ teaspoon salt

1. Mix the flour, oil and salt. Add water and prepare a stiff dough. Knead well.
2. Divide the dough into 25 portions.
3. Roll out into thin puris and prick with a fork.
4. Arrange the puris on a baking tray.
5. Bake in a hot oven at 200°C for 10 minutes.

Health Information: This wholesome replacement for the traditional fried and greasy puri uses the superior fat reducing method of baking.

Per Puri: Calories 13 ● Protein 0.4g ● Carbohydrates 2.3g ● Fat 0.2g

1. CUCUMBER SNACK, page 115
2. SPICY SPINACH DUMPLINGS, page 66
3. TOMATO COCKTAIL CUPS, page 119
4. CURD CHEESE DIP, page 43
5. GREEN CHUTNEY, page 129
6. TOMATO APPLE DRINK, page 19

Tomato Cocktail Cups

PICTURE ON PAGE 117

Preparation time: 10 minutes ● No cooking ● Makes 12 cups.

3 large tomatoes
1 grated cucumber
½ teacup fresh curds, *page 134*
a dash of finely chopped green chilli
1 tablespoon crumbled paneer, *page 135*
salt to taste
fresh dill (suva) *or* chopped coriander for decoration

1. Cut out sides 1 and 2 of each tomato as shown in the accompanying sketch. Then turn around and cut out sides 3 and 4. Scoop out the pulp from each side so that firm tomato cups are left.
2. Squeeze out water from the cucumber.
3. Add the curds, green chilli, paneer and salt and mix.
4. Fill the tomato cups with this mixture and place in the refrigerator.

★ Decorate with dill and serve cold.

Health Information: Use this low-calorie snack for cocktails instead of high-calorie accompaniments like nuts and fried snacks.

Per Cup: Calories 11 ● Protein 1g ● Carbohydrates 1.5g ● Fat 0.1g

1. STEWED PEARS WITH ORANGE SAUCE, page 103
2. VANILLA SQUARES WITH STRAWBERRY SAUCE, page 99
3. FRUITY SALAD, page 102

Open Sandwiches

Preparation time: 5 minutes ● Cooking time: 5 minutes ● Makes 3 sandwiches.

3   brown bread slices, *page 133*

For the paneer spread
50 grams crumbled paneer, *page 135*
1   tablespoon fresh curds, *page 134*
a dash of finely chopped green chilli
salt to taste

1. Mix all the ingredients for the spread.
2. Divide into three equal parts and apply on each bread slice.

★ Serve as open sandwiches.

Health Information: A healthy breakfast or snack with the flavour of cheese. Low in calories.

Per Serving: Calories 98 ● Protein 8g ● Carbohydrates 15g ● Fat 0.8g

For the spinach spread
10 to 12 steamed spinach leaves
1   tablespoon crumbled paneer, *page 135*
a dash of finely chopped green chilli
salt to taste

Health Information: A healthy breakfast or snack of high fibre whole wheat bread and mineral rich spinach which is energy giving and satisfying.

Per Serving: Calories 85 ● Protein 5g ● Carbohydrates 15g ● Fat 0.7g

Carrot Sprouts Sandwich

Preparation time: 10 minutes • No cooking • Makes 1 sandwich.

1 teaspoon carrot butter, *page 134*
1 tablespoon crumbled paneer, *page 135*
a dash of finely chopped green chilli
1 brown bread slice, *page 133*
¼ teacup bean sprouts, *page 136* or alfalfa
   sprouts, *page 131*
salt to taste

1. Apply the carrot butter on one side of the bread slice.
2. Mix the crumbled paneer with the green chilli and salt and apply on the buttered side.
3. Spread the sprouts on top.

   ★ Cut into 4 pieces and serve.

Health Information: A well balanced and nutritious dish which is rich in vitamins and minerals as well as high in proteins and complex carbohydrates.

Per Sandwich: Calories 170 • Protein 12g • Carbohydrates 26g • Fat 2g

---

Carrot and Paneer Toast

PICTURE ON PAGE 71

Preparation time: 10 minutes • Cooking time: 5 minutes • Makes 3 toasts.

3 brown bread slices, *page 133*
1 teacup grated carrot
50 grams grated paneer, *page 135*
1 tablespoon finely chopped tomato
¼ teaspoon chopped green chilli
1 teaspoon chopped coriander
1 teaspoon butter
salt to taste

1. Toast the bread slices.
2. Mix the carrot, paneer, tomato, green chilli, coriander, butter and salt. Divide into three.
3. Place one portion of the mixture on each toast. Heat in an oven for a few minutes.

   ★ Serve hot.

Health Information: A vitamin-rich breakfast or snack made with whole wheat bread.

Per Toast: Calories 133 • Protein 8g • Carbohydrates 21g • Fat 2.2g

Spicy Moong Dal Waffles

PICTURE ON PAGE 127

Preparation time: 10 minutes ● Cooking time: 15 minutes ● Serves 4.

1 teacup moong dal with skin
2 to 3 chopped green chillies
2 tablespoons chopped fenugreek (methi) leaves
2 teaspoons gram flour (besan)
a pinch asafoetida
¼ teaspoon soda bi-carb
2 pinches sugar (optional)
2 teaspoons oil
salt to taste

Accompaniment
green chutney, *page 129*

1. Soak the moong dal in water for 3 to 4 hours. Then wash it very well.
2. Blend the soaked dal in a blender with the green chillies and a little water.
3. Add the fenugreek leaves, gram flour, asafoetida, soda bi-carb, sugar, oil and salt and mix well.
4. Pour a little batter at a time in a preheated waffle iron and bake until crisp. Repeat for the remaining batter.

★ Serve hot with green chutney.

Variation 1: MOONG DAL AND METHI DHOKLAS Instead of soda bi-carb, use ½ teaspoon of fruit salt. At step 4, pour the batter immediately into a 225 or 250 mm. diameter well greased thali and steam for 5 minutes. Serve as above.

Variation 2: MOONG DAL AND METHI PANKIS Spread a little batter very thinly on a well greased non-stick frying pan. Cook on both sides. Serve as above.

Health Information: Moong dal with the skin on retains all the B group vitamins during cooking. This recipe replaces the traditional cooking method for preparing snacks (e.g. frying in case of moong dal bhajias) by the healthier method of cooking using the dry heat of a waffle iron.

Per Serving: Calories 131 ● Protein 7g ● Carbohydrates 19g ● Fat 3.5g

Russian Sandwich

PICTURE ON PAGE 90

Preparation time: 10 minutes • No cooking • Makes 4 sandwiches.

4   brown bread slices, *page 133*

For the sandwich filling
1   teacup finely chopped boiled
    vegetables (carrots, cabbage, green
    peas, cauliflower, potatoes, french
    beans)
3   to 4 tablespoons fresh cream, *page 126*
2   teaspoons thick fresh curds, *page 134*
2   tablespoons grated carrots
1   teaspoon mustard powder
½   teaspoon sugar
1   teaspoon salt
a pinch pepper powder

For topping
cress

1. Mix all the ingredients for the
   sandwich filling.
2. Divide the mixture into two and
   spread over 2 slices of bread.
3. Cover with the other 2 slices.

★ Cut each sandwich into two,
decorate with cress and serve.

Health Information: The high fat and cholesterol containing mayonnaise is replaced in this sandwich by fresh cream and curds, thereby providing a healthy snack, rich in many essential minerals.

Per Sandwich: Calories 102 • Protein 5g • Carbohydrates 19g • Fat 0.8g

Bhel

Preparation time: 10 minutes ● No cooking ● Serves 2.

6 baked puris, *page 116*
2 tablespoons boiled moong, preferably
   sprouted, *page 131*
1 teacup puffed rice (kurmure)
1 teacup fresh curds, *page 134*
1 chopped onion
1 chopped tomato
3 tablespoons sweet and sour chutney,
   page 132
3 tablespoons green chutney, *page 129*
1 teaspoon chopped fresh green mango
   (optional)
salt to taste

For topping
1 tablespoon chopped coriander

1. Crush the puris.
2. Add the remaining ingredients and
   mix.

★ Serve immediately in individual
dishes topped with coriander.

Note: Adjust the quantities of the
chutnies to taste.

Health Information: This unusual bhel is much more than a snack! It makes a
healthy balanced meal because it is very rich in proteins, complex carbohydrates,
vitamins, iron and calcium.

Per Serving: Calories 182 ● Protein 10g ● Carbohydrates 33g ● Fat 1.5g

9. Basic Recipes

Vanilla Cream

Preparation time: 5 minutes • Cooking time: 10 minutes • Makes 3 cups.

6 teaspoons chopped China grass
3 teacups skim milk, *page 132*
6 teaspoons sugar
½ teaspoon vanilla essence
cut fruit *or* jelly pieces to serve

1. Add ¾ teacup of water to the China grass and cook on a slow flame until it dissolves completely. Strain.
2. Boil the milk and add the China grass and sugar.
3. Allow to cool to room temperature and then add the vanilla essence.
4. Pour the mixture into a bowl and put to set in the refrigerator.
5. Just before serving, beat up the lightly set cream.

★ Serve with fruit and jelly pieces.

Health Information: A delightful low cholesterol low fat alternative to cream which nevertheless provides adequate proteins and B12 Vitamins.

Per Cup: Calories 93 • Protein 7g • Carbohydrates 16g • Fat 0g

Fresh Cream

Preparation time: a few minutes ● No cooking ● Serves 6.

100 grams fresh paneer, *page 135*
3   tablespoons skim milk, *page 132*

Use the freshly made moist paneer immediately after step 2 of the procedure on *page 135*.
Put the paneer and milk in a liquidiser and churn until creamy.

Note: Add sugar to taste to obtain sweetened fresh cream.

Variation: STRAWBERRIES WITH CREAM Use 3 teacups of fresh, sliced strawberries and 4 teaspoons of sugar in addition to above recipe. Mix the strawberries, cream and sugar and serve cold. Alternatively, mix the strawberries with vanilla cream, *page 125*, to taste and serve cold.

Health Information: A wonderful alternative to rich fresh cream which is high in calories and cholesterol and fat. It makes desserts lighter without compromising taste.

Per Serving: Calories 229 ● Protein 38g ● Carbohydrates 15g ● Fat 1.5g

1. SPICY MOONG DAL WAFFLES, page 122
2. MINI PIZZAS, page 112
3. COFFEE FRAPPÉ, page 16

Tomato Gravy

Preparation time: 10 minutes • Cooking time: 10 minutes • Makes 2 cups.

4 chopped tomatoes
1 chopped onion
2 cloves crushed garlic (optional)
½ teaspoon chilli powder
1 teaspoon sugar (optional)
2 teaspoons oil
salt to taste

1. Heat the oil and fry the onions and garlic for 1 minute.
2. Add the tomatoes and cook until soft.
3. Blend in a liquidiser.
4. Add the chilli powder, sugar and salt and boil for 2 to 3 minutes.

Health Information: A delicious accompanying sauce for many Western dishes. Rich in Vitamins A, C and K and chromium, it is good for the complexion too.

Per Cup: Calories 98 • Protein 2g • Carbohydrates 10.5g • Fat 5.5g

---

White Sauce

Preparation time: a few minutes • Cooking time: 15 minutes • Makes 3 cups.

2 teacups cauliflower *or* white pumpkin (lauki)
2 teaspoons butter
1 tablespoon whole wheat *or* plain flour
1 teacup skim milk, *page 132*
salt and pepper to taste

1. Boil the cauliflower in 2 teacups of water until soft. Blend in a liquidiser and strain.
2. Heat the butter, add the flour and cook for ½ minute.
3. Add the milk and cauliflower purée and heat whilst stirring the mixture continuously until it becomes thick.
4. Add salt and pepper.

Health Information: The recipe uses cauliflower as a thickening agent. It is low in calories but rich in Vitamin C and is a nutritious alternative to the usual white sauce (which uses more of refined flour and butter for thickening).

Per Cup: Calories 82 • Protein 4g • Carbohydrates 10g • Fat 3g

130

Green Chutney

PICTURE ON PAGE 128

Preparation time: 5 minutes ● No cooking ● Makes 1 cup.

1 teacup chopped coriander
4 chopped green chillies
2 tablespoons grated fresh coconut *or*
   roasted gram dal
1 teaspoon lemon juice
½ teaspoon sugar
½ teaspoon salt

1. Mix the coriander, green chillies, coconut, sugar, salt and 2 teaspoons of water.
2. Add the lemon juice.
3. Blend in a liquidiser.

Health Information: An excellent recipe which gives a large portion of the recommended dietary intake of iron and Vitamin C. This can be served with savoury snacks for enhancing the taste and food value of the dish.

Per Cup: Calories 145 ● Protein 8g ● Carbohydrates 24g ● Fat 2g

1. BAKED PURIS, page 116
2. SPROUTED MOONG SALAD, page 38
3. CURDS, page 134
4. SWEET AND SOUR CHUTNEY, page 132
5. GREEN CHUTNEY, page 129

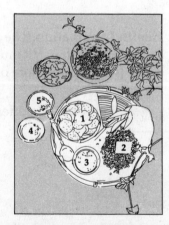

Sprouted Pulses

Preparation time: 1 day • No cooking.

100 grams moong, matki, chana, peas etc.

1. Wash the pulses and soak in water for 5 to 6 hours.
2. Drain the water and put the soaked pulses in a bowl. Cover with a piece of cloth. Do not tie the pulses in the cloth. Leave overnight.

Health Information: Every seed which is suitable for sprouting is a miniature storehouse of nutrients. The Vitamin C content of moong is greatly increased by soaking them in water and allowing germination.

Sweet and Sour Sauce

Preparation time: 5 minutes • Cooking time: 4 minutes • Makes 1 cup.

2 tomatoes
1 tablespoon vinegar
½ teaspoon soya sauce
1 teaspoon chilli sauce
2 teaspoons sugar
1 teaspoon cornflour
salt to taste

1. Put the tomatoes in hot water for 10 minutes. Grate.
2. Mix the tomato pulp with the remaining ingredients and add 1 tablespoon of water.
3. Boil until thick. Cool. Store in the refrigerator.

Health Information: A vitamin-rich sauce which imparts a piquant flavour to the dish.

Per Cup: Calories 80 • Protein 2g • Carbohydrates 19g • Fat 0.4g

Skim Milk

Preparation time: 5 minutes • Cooking time: 7 minutes • Makes 5 cups.

100 grams skim milk powder
1 litre water

1. Mix the skim milk powder in 1½ cups of water and make a smooth paste.
2. Add the remaining water and if desired, beat with an egg beater.
3. Boil.

Note: Every packet of skim milk has different methods of preparation. The above is given by way of guidance and the instructions on the packet should be followed.

Health Information: Skim milk has all the goodness of milk without fat.

Per Cup: Calories 72 • Protein 7g • Carbohydrates 10.4g • Fat 0g

Sweet and Sour Chutney

PICTURE ON PAGE 128

Preparation time: a few minutes • Cooking time: 5 minutes • Makes 1 cup.

25 grams tamarind (imli)
30 grams dates
4 teaspoons sugar
½ teaspoon chilli powder
½ teaspoon cumin powder
¼ teaspoon salt
a pinch black salt (sanchal) (optional)

1. Wash the tamarind and dates and remove the seeds.
2. Boil the tamarind, dates, sugar and salt with 1½ teacups of water for 5 minutes.
3. Blend the mixture in a mixer and strain.
4. Add the chilli powder, cumin powder and black salt and mix well.

Health Information: A mineral-rich accompaniment for added taste and flavour.

Per Cup: Calories 198 • Protein 1.5g • Carbohydrates 44g • Fat 2g

Brown Bread

Preparation time: 1 hour (including proving) ● Cooking time: 25 minutes ● Makes 13 slices *or* 6 buns.

250 grams whole wheat flour
10 grams fresh yeast
¾ teaspoon sugar
1 teaspoon butter
¾ teaspoon salt

1. Sieve the flour. Make a well in the centre.
2. Add the yeast, sugar and a little warm water.
3. Wait for at least 4 to 5 minutes *or* until bubbles come on top.
4. Add the butter and salt.
5. Make a soft dough by adding some more warm water.
6. Knead for 2 minutes. Leave for 20 minutes and knead again for a while.
7. Shape into a loaf and press into a greased loaf tin with your fingers. If you wish to make buns or small loaves, shape accordingly and arrange on a greased baking tin.
8. Wait for at least 25 minutes *or* until double in size.
9. Bake in a hot oven at 200°C for 10 minutes.
10. Then reduce the temperature to 150°C and bake further for 15 minutes.

Health Information: Brown bread is more nutritious than white bread as whole wheat flour contains more protein, minerals, vitamins and fibre than processed white flour.

Per bread slice: Calories 70 ● Protein 3g ● Carbohydrates 14g ● Fat 1g

Fresh Curds

Preparation time: 5 minutes • Setting time: 4 to 5 hours • Makes 5 cups.

1   litre skim milk, *page 132*
1   tablespoon curds (made the previous day)

1. Warm the milk.
2. Add the curds, beat up the mixture and cover.
3. Keep aside until the curds set (approximately 5 to 6 hours). During the cold climate, place inside a cupboard or closed oven to set.

Health Information: Curds have all the nutritive value of milk and when eaten with dishes like parathas or rice, they complement the proteins present in these foods to make it a complete protein. They have good proteins, vitamins and calcium and are considered the world over as a nutritious addition to the diet.

Per Cup: Calories 63 • Protein 8g • Carbohydrates 6g • Fat 1g

Carrot Butter

Preparation time: 5 minutes • No cooking • Makes 3 tablespoons.

2   tablespoons grated carrots
1   tablespoon butter
a little mustard powder
salt to taste

1. Add a few drops of water to the mustard powder and mix well.
2. After 5 minutes, add to the butter and grated carrots.
3. Add salt.

Note: Use this butter as a spread for sandwiches and toasts.

Variation: PARSLEY BUTTER Use 2 tablespoons of chopped parsley instead of carrots and follow the same procedure.

Health Information: Carrots provide Vitamin A and impart an interesting flavour. This recipe decreases the amount of butter to be used and makes a great spread.

Per Tablespoon: Calories 39 • Protein 0g • Carbohydrates 1g • Fat 4g

Paneer

Preparation time: 5 minutes • Cooking time: 10 minutes • Makes 100 grams.

1 litre skim milk, *page 132*
juice of 1 lemon *or* 1 cup curds, *page 134*

1. Put the milk to boil. When it starts boiling, remove from the heat and wait for 2 to 3 minutes. Then, add the lemon juice and stir gently till all the milk curdles.
2. Leave covered for some time. Then, pour over a thin muslin cloth and drain out the whey.
3. Cover with a cloth and place a weight on top to drain out the water.

★ Cut into pieces or crumble as required

Note: Use of curds gives smoother paneer.

Health Information: This type of paneer has a lot of proteins with very little fat. It is also rich in Vitamin B12, calcium, phosphorous and zinc.

Per 100gm Serving: Calories 158 • Protein 30g • Carbohydrates 8g • Fat 1g

Bean Sprouts

Preparation time: 2 days ● No cooking ● Makes 3 cups.

1 teacup moong beans

1. Wash the moong and soak in water for a minimum 4 hours.
2. Drain thoroughly and wait for 5 minutes.
3. Keep in a jar covered with a piece of cloth for 5 to 6 hours.
4. Place in the refrigerator overnight.
5. Next day, wash thoroughly, drain and again keep in a jar covered with a piece of cloth for 5 to 6 hours.
6. Place in the refrigerator overnight.
7. Sprinkle water on the sprouted beans on the third day and store in the refrigerator until required for use.

Health Information: In the process of sprouting, Vitamins A, B group and C (which are otherwise absent in ordinary moong beans) are formed. Beans are very rich in proteins, complex carbohydrates and iron.

Per Cup: Calories 167 ● Protein 12g ● Carbohydrates 28g ● Fat 0.6g

NUTRITIONAL CHART

RECIPE	CALORIES	PROTEINS	FATS	CARBOHYDRATE	FIBRE	VIT. A	VIT. B1	VIT. B2	VIT. B6	VIT. B12	VIT. C	FOLIC ACID	IRON	CALCIUM	PHOSPHORUS

I. DRINKS

RECIPE	CALORIES	PROTEINS	FATS	CARBOHYDRATE	FIBRE	VIT. A	VIT. B1	VIT. B2	VIT. B6	VIT. B12	VIT. C	FOLIC ACID	IRON	CALCIUM	PHOSPHORUS
FROSTED TOMATO COCKTAIL, page 15	60					■					■				
COFFEE FRAPPÉ, page 16	52							■					■		
TOMATO APPLE DRINK, page 19	40					■									
HEALTH DRINK, page 20	69		■								■				
GOLDEN GLOW, page 20	42					■					■				
ICY WATERMELON DRINK, page 21	56														
SUNSHINE DRINK, page 21	72		■												
MINTY CUCUMBER COOLER, page 22	52							■					■		
FRUIT CUP, page 22	60		■												

II. SOUPS

RECIPE	CALORIES	PROTEINS	FATS	CARBOHYDRATE	FIBRE	VIT. A	VIT. B1	VIT. B2	VIT. B6	VIT. B12	VIT. C	FOLIC ACID	IRON	CALCIUM	PHOSPHORUS
SPINACH SOUP, page 23	55	■				■					■			■	■
LENTIL SOUP, page 24	101	■		■											
CAULIFLOWER SOUP, page 25	57	■													■
LENTIL AND SPINACH SOUP, page 26	48														
CHINESE CLEAR VEGETABLE SOUP, page 27	63					■									
CARROT SOUP, page 28	60					■									
MOONG DAL AND SPINACH SOUP, page 28	48														
GAZPACHO, page 29	59			■	■						■				
CLEAR VEGETABLE BROTH, page 30	77					■									
MUSHROOM SOUP, page 30	31														
CURD SHORBA, page 31	98	■						■						■	
MIXED VEGETABLE SOUP, page 31	27														
COLD CUCUMBER SOUP, page 32	76	■						■						■	
VEGETABLE SOUP, page 33	89	■		■											
GREEN PEAS SKIN SOUP, page 34	55	■		■											

III. SALADS

RECIPE	CALORIES	PROTEINS	FATS	CARBOHYDRATE	FIBRE	VIT. A	VIT. B1	VIT. B2	VIT. B6	VIT. B12	VIT. C	FOLIC ACID	IRON	CALCIUM	PHOSPHORUS
SLIMMERS' SALAD, page 37	72			■	■	■									
SPROUTED MOONG SALAD, page 38	53	■			■										
BEAN SPROUTS SALAD, page 39	85	■													
STUFFED CAPSICUMS, page 39	31										■				

 LARGE AMOUNT    MODERATE AMOUNT   LITTLE OR NONE

	CALORIES	PROTEINS	FATS	CARBOHYDRATE	FIBRE	VIT. A	VIT. B1	VIT. B2	VIT. B6	VIT. B12	VIT. C	FOLIC ACID	IRON	CALCIUM	PHOSPHORUS

RECIPE

III. SALADS (continued)

RECIPE	
FRUITY BEAN SALAD, page 40	62
FRUITY VEGETABLE SALAD, page 41	53
ORANGE AND CABBAGE SALAD, page 42	52

IV. DIPS, DRESSINGS AND RAITA

RECIPE	
CURD CHEESE DIP, page 43	34
FRUIT AND VEGETABLE RAITA, page 44	27
THOUSAND ISLAND CURDS DRESSING, page 44	15
SPINACH RAITA, page 45	18
CURD DRESSING, page 45	76
EGG PLANT DIP, page 46	27

V. INDIAN DISHES

RECIPE	
BAKED VEGETABLE JALFRAZIE, page 47	86
SPINACH AND VEGETABLE DELIGHT, page 48	66
PANEER METHI PALAK, page 49	88
DAL WITH SPINACH, page 50	90
NAWABI CURRY, page 51	66
TOMATO AND CAULIFLOWER CURRY, page 52	67
BRINJAL BHURTA, page 55	69
PLAIN PARATHAS, page 56	54
SPINACH STUFFING FOR PLAIN PARATHAS, page 57	25
CAULIFLOWER STUFFING FOR PLAIN PARATHAS, page 57	15
CABBAGE STUFFING FOR PLAIN PARATHAS, page 58	10
CHINESE STUFFING FOR PLAIN PARATHAS, page 58	39
STUFFED BAJRA ROTI, page 59	115
MINTY STUFFED PARATHAS, page 60	91
PANEER PALAK METHI ROTIS, page 62	90
RICE AND MOONG DAL IDLI, page 63	66
SUJI IDLI, page 64	8
MOONG DAL DHOKLAS, page 65	36
SPICY SPINACH DUMPLINGS, page 66	17

■ LARGE AMOUNT   ▨ MODERATE AMOUNT   ☐ LITTLE OR NONE

RECIPE	CALORIES	PROTEINS	FATS	CARBOHYDRATE	FIBRE	VIT. A	VIT. B1	VIT. B2	VIT. B6	VIT. B12	VIT. C	FOLIC ACID	IRON	CALCIUM	PHOSPHORUS

V. INDIAN DISHES (continued)

RECIPE	CALORIES
MOONG DAL DAHI WADAS, page 67	61
MOONG DAL PANKI, page 68	28
MASOOR DAL WITH RICE, page 69	188
MOONG MISAL, page 70	87
PUMPKIN HANDVA, page 73	79
CAULIFLOWER WITH CHUTNEY, page 74	92
SPICY TOMATO RASAM, page 75	25
MIXED PULSES WITH VEGETABLES, page 76	88

VI. WESTERN DISHES

RECIPE	CALORIES
CABBAGE ROLLS, page 77	130
BAKED PANEER IN SPINACH WITH TOMATO GRAVY, page 78	108
VEGETABLE FLORENTINE, page 79	101
SIZZLER, page 80	586
SPINACH AND PANEER IN TOMATO GRAVY, page 81	67
MIXED VEGETABLES IN CREAMY SAUCE, page 81	113
BAKED CANNELONI, page 82	113
STUFFED CABBAGE LEAVES WITH SPINACH, page 83	37
STUFFED SPINACH LEAVES IN WHITE SAUCE, page 84	89
WHOLE WHEAT PASTA WITH TOMATO GRAVY, page 85	240
INDIAN VEGETABLE BARBEQUE, page 86	183
BAKED STUFFED TOMATOES, page 87	58
BAKED TOMATO SLICES, page 88	39
TOMATO CUPS WITH COTTAGE CHEESE, page 91	70
CORN STUFFED POTATO, page 92	136
TOMATOES STUFFED WITH BEANS SPROUTS, page 93	98
CHINESE STIR FRIED VEGETABLES, page 94	388

VII. DESSERTS

RECIPE	CALORIES
STRAWBERRY YOGHURT, page 95	78
HAWAIIAN FRUIT BOWL, page 96	82
APPLE SLICES WITH VANILLA CREAM, page 97	74

■ LARGE AMOUNT   ▨ MODERATE AMOUNT   ☐ LITTLE OR NONE

Columns (left to right): CALORIES, PROTEINS, FATS, CARBOHYDRATE, FIBRE, VIT. A, VIT. B1, VIT. B2, VIT. B6, VIT. B12, VIT. C, FOLIC ACID, IRON, CALCIUM, PHOSPHORUS

RECIPE

VII. DESSERTS (continued)

Recipe	Calories
PAPAYA PUDDING, page 97	26
SAFFRON CARDAMOM SQUARES, page 98	48
SANDESH, page 99	57
APPLE ROLL WITH VANILLA CREAM, page 100	122
KESARI SWEET CURDS, page 101	65
APPLE WHIP, page 101	61
FRUIT SALAD, page 102	80
BAKED APPLE SURPRISE, page 102	68
STEWED PEARS WITH ORANGE SAUCE, page 103	75
APPLES AND SAFFRON SAUCE, page 104	100
STUFFED APPLES IN SAFFRON SAUCE, page 105	83
ORANGE SAUCE, page 106	116

VIII. SNACKS

Recipe	Calories
MUSHROOM AND TOMATO SNACK, page 109	66
SALSA DIP, page 110	42
LETTUCE CUPS, page 111	16
MINI PIZZAS, page 112	75
WHOLE WHEAT BURGERS, page 114	147
CUCUMBER SNACK, page 115	29
MASALA PURI, page 115	18
BAKED PURI, page 116	13
TOMATO COCKTAIL CUPS, page 119	11
OPEN SANDWICHES — PANEER, page 120	98
OPEN SANDWICHES — SPINACH, page 120	85
CARROT SPROUTS SANDWICH, page 121	170
CARROT AND PANEER TOAST, page 121	133
SPICY MOONG DAL WAFFLES, page 122	131
RUSSIAN SANDWICH, page 123	102
BHEL, page 124	182

■ LARGE AMOUNT   ▨ MODERATE AMOUNT   ☐ LITTLE OR NONE